# TEENS PARENTING

Other Books by Jeanne Warren Lindsay:

*Teens Parenting—Your Baby's First Year*
*Do I Have a Daddy? A Story About a Single-Parent Child*
*School-Age Parents: Challenge of Three-Generation Living*
*Teenage Marriage: Coping with Reality*
*Teens Look at Marriage: Rainbows, Roles and Reality*
*Parents, Pregnant Teens and the Adoption Option*
*Pregnant Too Soon: Adoption Is an Option*
*Open Adoption: A Caring Option*

By Jeanne Lindsay and Jean Brunelli:

*Teens Parenting—Your Pregnancy and Newborn Journey*

By Jeanne Lindsay and Sally McCullough:

*Teens Parenting—Discipline from Birth to Three*

By Jeanne Lindsay and Sharon Rodine:

*Teen Pregnancy Challenge, Book One:*
*Strategies for Change*

*Teen Pregnancy Challenge, Book Two:*
*Programs for Kids*

By Jeanne Lindsay and Catherine Monserrat:

*Adoption Awareness: A Guide for Teachers,*
*Counselors, Nurses and Caring Others*

TEENS PARENTING

# THE CHALLENGE
# OF TODDLERS

## Parenting Your Child
## from One to Three

Jeanne Warren Lindsay, MA, CHE

Morning
Glory
Press

**Buena Park, California**

*Teens Parenting—The Challenge of Toddlers*
is part of a four-book series. Other titles are:
*Teens Parenting—Your Pregnancy and Newborn Journey*
*Teens Parenting—Your Baby's First Year*
*Teens Parenting—Discipline from Birth to Three*

Library of Congress Cataloging-in-Publication Data

Lindsay, Jeanne Warren.
    Teens parenting : the challenge of toddlers : parenting your child
from one to three / Jeanne Warren Lindsay
    192 p.   cm.
    Includes bibliographical references and index.
    Summary: Describes for teenage parents the development and
special needs of children from one to three.
    ISBN 0-930934-59-8 : $15.95.  -- ISBN 0-930934-58-x (pbk.) :
$9.95
    1. Toddlers--United States--Juvenile literature. 2. Child rearing--
United States--Juvenile literature. 3. Teenage parents--United States-
-Juvenile literature. [1. Teenage parents. 2. Parenting. 3. Child
development.]  I. Title.  II. Title: Challenge of toddlers.
HQ774.5.L56  1991
649'. 122--dc20                                              91-30316
                                                                  CIP
                                                                   AC

MORNING GLORY PRESS, INC.
6595 San Haroldo Way        Buena Park, CA 90620-3748
(714) 828-1998
Printed and bound in the United States of America

# Contents

# Acknowledgments

I am grateful to Julie Vetica, Sally McCullough, and Jean Brunelli who made time to read and critique this manuscript. Their comments were invaluable. I also appreciate the supportive comments from Sharon Herold and Ronda Simpson-Brown, and the lovely Foreword from Lois Gatchell.

Perhaps even more important is the input from pregnant and parenting teens, the young people we interviewed, and whose wisdom is scattered throughout the book. Sixty-seven young people are quoted, and many of them gave us permission to include their names.

They include Lissa Mosqueda, Albert Aguilar, Angela and Chris Cardena, Jessica Aguilar, Lorena Martinez Silva, Linda Solano, Karen Perlas Gagui, Jennifer Launchbury, Michelle Conway, Cynthia and Roman Mendoza, Rebecca Reeves, Deanne Andringa Grachen, Karen Smith Lind, Terri Emerson, Alicia Ochoa, Julie Farah, Lupe Cordi, Michelle Bragdon, Angelica Ramos, Tammy Peace, Judy Chavez, Dolores Cruz Corrales, Ardell Hucko, Cynthia Mendoza, Lynetta Allen, Jo Ann Harris, Anita Smith, Michelle Johnson, Gabriel and Tammy Ayala, and Larry Jaurequi.

We interviewed others who are quoted and acknowledged in the other books in the *Teens Parenting* series.

David Crawford, teacher in the Teen Mother Program, William Daylor High School, Sacramento, supplied most of the photographs. His models were his wonderful students. Also included (author's pay-off) are a couple of Lindsay grandchildren. In addition, a few of the photos were taken by Barbara Hellstrom and Cheryl Boeller.

Tim Rinker is the cover artist, and Steve Lindsay helped design the book. We appreciate so much the contributions of all of these talented people.

Carole Blum and Marlene Boehm again helped with the proof-reading and kept Morning Glory Press alive and well during book production time.

Thank you, Bob, for being supportive and caring no matter what else is going on in our lives. I love you very.

Jeanne Lindsay

# Preface

If you've been a parent for at least a year—or if you will be the parent of a child aged one to three, this book is for you. It's especially for you if you're a teenage parent.

Teenage mothers and fathers share their parenting insights throughout these pages. They speak from their realities, the realities of teenagers who are also parents. They share their dreams and their frustrations, their hopes and fears for their children and themselves.

Child-rearing is not the only topic discussed in these chapters. Tips for meeting your own needs are also offered. One of the most important things you can do for your child is to make a satisfying life for yourself as well as for him/her. You'll be able to parent better if your own life is going well. Caring for an active toddler may make it harder for you to follow your dreams. That's why it's even more important for you to make a plan now to start working toward those goals and those dreams.

During your baby's first year, you were probably absorbed in childcare. Caring for your baby was an all-consuming task. Your personal needs may have received little attention. By the time your baby is a year old, however, you may realize you need to get on with your own life, even as you continue caring for your child.

This book provides a guide for caring for children aged one to three years. It covers such topics as child development, nutrition, sleep, language development, health and safety, and activities for toddlers. Throughout, comments from young parents reinforce the concepts presented.

Other chapters focus on the needs of teen parents themselves. While the entire book is directed to both mothers and fathers, two chapters discuss two-parent issues specifically. "Dad's Ahead If He's Involved" advocates for strong two-parent cooperation in child-rearing when feasible, whether or not the parents are living together.

Teenage parents may be married to each other, they may be "together" but living apart, or one or both may be with a different partner. "The Partnership Challenge" provides a discussion of these various relationships. Young parents share insights gained from their experience with partners.

A chapter focuses on the teen parent's extended family, and another on planning one's family. The final chapter provides suggestions for you as you plan your future life. The importance of continuing your education, obtaining job skills, and becoming independent is emphasized.

Parenting a toddler is a difficult task for parents of any age. Combine this task with the special needs of adolescents, and it becomes a gigantic challenge. I hope this book will help you in your quest for a satisfying life for yourself even as you parent your toddler.

Jeanne Warren Lindsay                        September, 1991

# Foreword

I wish there had been a Jeanne Lindsay in my life in the late 1940s when I was having babies. Although I was a college graduate, married to a loving, supportive husband, I felt parenthood was the most important job I had ever undertaken, yet the one for which I was least prepared. I could have used the practical insights that Lindsay passes on to young parents that are reassuring, challenging, and fun.

Ideally, parenting should be enjoyed, as well as understood. This is not easy if the pregnancy was unplanned, unwanted. But the bond that a young woman usually begins to develop with the fetus becomes full blown when a new human being emerges from her labor.

Most of us can deal with the infant stage, because we love to feel needed. A cuddly infant is dependent, and

gradually grows responsive to our display of affection—
most rewarding! But when that infant turns into an active
toddler with the curiosity of an explorer, the imagination of
an artist, and the rebelliousness of an adolescent, watch out.
This is when the understanding, tact, challenge, patience,
and yes, endurance, of mothers and fathers is summoned.

If we parents cultivate these characteristics, then we find
the *joy* of watching a unique personality unfold before our
eyes. With eyes to see and ears to hear, we are privileged to
be part of the world of very interesting little people. This is
apparent in Lindsay's book. Whether she is dealing with
motor skills, feeding, bedtime, safety, active play, or
planning for the future, there is the fun of the present
developmental stage as well as the hope of the good life
to come.

When I was director of the Margaret Hudson Program
for teenage parents in Tulsa, Oklahoma, I found the fun of
the hundreds of babies with whom we dealt was their
differences. Surely there were common aspects of development, but also very early they had distinct personalities.

These babies enriched the parents, the staff, and each
other as they learned to respond to their environment. We
had the sense of being potters, experimenting with lumps of
human clay. I, for one, would find myself praying to my
God, "Oh, Lord, make me a worthy potter of this precious
little vessel."

The teen mothers quoted in this book are confronting
the realities of parenthood. One would hope that they, and
those who come after, would find the supports in our
society that provide the needed guidance and encourage-
ment to produce competent, healthy children. *The
Challenge of Toddlers* is one of these supports.

(The Reverend) Lois H. Gatchell
Deacon, Episcopal Diocese of Oklahoma

To the young parents who shared so freely
and taught me so much
as we worked together.

*Your child is an exciting challenge.*

# CHAPTER 1

# He's One—Soon He'll Be Running

*Heidi loves to go to the park. She notices little bugs on the ground, little ants. She'll put her face down close to them, make her little noises, and show me.*

*She has a little bug catcher toy. When I put a bug in it, she picks it up and looks at it. Then I let the bug go.*

*I take her for a walk each evening. I teach her things on the way. We stop every day and look at two dogs and some parakeets behind a fence down the street. One day the owner showed us his birds. She was thrilled.*

Jenny, 18 - Heidi, 13 months

*Alice takes off her socks and shoes. She'll put her shirt on. She likes to play peek-a-boo with it. If I'm*

*putting a shirt on, she'll pick up anything around,*
*maybe a nightgown, and put her head through the*
*hole. Then she laughs.*

Melanie, 15 - Alice, 13 months

At your child's first birthday you may be startled at the
changes you observe in each of you. Your child has developed from a helpless newborn to a whirlwind little person
who scoots everywhere and either is walking or will
be soon.

Even more wonderful than his physical development are
the tremendous jumps in his "knowledge bank." He's
learning many new things each day, and will continue to
progress rapidly with living, learning, and loving under
your guidance.

*Now Alice climbs off beds and is learning how to*
*climb up on the bed. I bought her a little skate toy*
*when she was one year old. Within a month, she*
*learned how to get on and off it. She also tried to stop*
*it from going anywhere by climbing on top of it.*

Melanie

She is learning to walk, which gives her a lovely feeling
of independence. She can ride simple wheel toys such as
kiddie-cars. She's discovered that by climbing she can find
even more places to explore. She can easily get herself into
serious trouble if no one is watching.

He has become more interested in toys like shape boxes,
form boards, blocks and balls. He especially enjoys these
things if someone is nearby to watch or play with him. He
enjoys crayons or paints when he is allowed to use them.

She is beginning to talk. She is learning to tell you what
she wants through words and gestures. She can follow
simple directions. But any understanding of right and
wrong, the ability to make simple judgments about

behavior, will not even begin to emerge until she is close to two. Even then she often won't know or understand what she should or shouldn't do.

You, too, have probably changed a great deal during your child's first year. Do you feel only a couple of years older than you were BP (Before Pregnancy)? Or are you convinced that you've grown up—matured—at a far faster pace than your birthdays indicate? If you think you're more mature than your actual years, you're probably right. The responsibilities of parenting for both mothers and fathers are awesome.

> *The hardest part for me was the change when Cassandra was born. I couldn't be myself any more. I couldn't stay young and irresponsible.*
>
> *It was hard when we moved out when she was 14 months old. My mom was always there doing stuff for me, and Cassandra was in the infant center while I was at school. I didn't really have a chance to see what it was like on my own until we moved.*
>
> *Her father helps me out, but taking care of Cassie is still my responsibility. It's an amazing amount of responsibility. It's also amazing how my love for her has grown since I've been raising her on my own.*
>
> Kris, 17 - Cassandra, 25 months

Perhaps the biggest change you'll experience with your child during these toddler years is her individuality and independence. When she was an infant, it was generally your job to decide what was best for her. Now she will insist more and more on making her own decisions.

## Walking Adds Excitement

Once your baby starts walking, he's considered a toddler. Being able to walk adds a lot of excitement to his life.

He can explore even more than he could by crawling, no matter how rapidly he was traveling through your home. He can move faster, reach higher, and enjoy life even more.

*Heidi has been walking since she was 10 months old, and she started taking steps at 8 months. You tell her to come here, and she'll turn around and go the other way. She's very good at ignoring you. If she's entering the negative stage, she's getting good at it!*

Jenny

Starting to walk at ten months is unusual. Most children wait until they're 12 to 14 months old, and some are even older when they take those first steps. If you're nervous because your 17-month-old son isn't walking yet, talk with your doctor.

Your child will probably cruise from one piece of furniture to another, perhaps for several weeks, before he starts walking on his own. When he finally walks, his balance and coordination won't be well developed. He'll stretch his arms out to his sides and walk with his legs somewhat spread apart. At first he'll lean slightly forward and take short steps.

Soon his rhythm will improve. Sometime during this stage he'll be able to stoop down, pick something up, and carry it around. Notice how proud he is of this new talent.

Before long he will walk pulling or pushing a toy. This is the time for the corn popper or other push/pull toy. He much prefers a toy that makes a noise as he pulls or pushes it along.

He doesn't need shoes until he starts walking outside. In fact, walking barefoot helps strengthen his feet and arches.

When you buy shoes for him, be sure they fit well, look comfortable, and aren't too big. There should be about one-half inch of space between his big toe and the end of his shoe. You'll have to replace his shoes often because his

*He's learning to talk, but first he jabbers.*

feet will grow so quickly. As long as they fit well, it's all right to buy the cheapest brand of shoes you can find. Sneakers are fine.

## He Jabbers Before He Talks

Talking means jabbering at this stage. He may say his first word about the time of his first birthday. He will communicate mostly through gestures for awhile yet. He's eager to learn more words, so play the labeling game with him. Point to an object and name it, then wait for him to repeat the name. "Table." "Chair." "Kitty." He may try to say the word after you.

Will your child be bilingual? If two languages are spoken in your home, you probably will want him to learn both. Some people suggest that one parent or caregiver always speak one language to the child, and the other parent or caregiver speak the second language. They feel the child will be able to keep the two languages separate more easily when this happens.

*If you can teach your child to be bilingual,
you're giving him a valuable gift*

If he's learning two languages, his overall language ability may develop a little more slowly than will the language of a child learning only one. By the time he enters kindergarten, he should speak both languages well.

If you can teach your child to become bilingual, you're giving him a valuable gift.

## She Copies Mom and Dad

She likes to copy you. She may feed you pieces of her food, then smile broadly if you take it. She probably loves having you copy her. You can copy her movements and her play activities. She's likely to be delighted.

Copying you is one of her best learning techniques. If you stack a block on top of another, she may do the same thing. If you demonstrate drinking from a cup, she may learn a little more quickly. Her speech, of course, depends a great deal on your modeling.

*Alice likes to try to write, perhaps because I've been writing a lot of letters this year and she likes to watch me. She knows keys go in the ignition, and she'll try to do that.*

Melanie

Your toddler may enjoy showing off. Her sense of humor may be developing nicely:

*Alice makes faces at me, sniffles her nose, laughs. If she does something people like and they laugh, she grins real big. Lots of times when she does something we like, we clap. Then she starts clapping for herself.*

Melanie

Letting her know you like what she's doing is the best way to help her develop a good sense of self-esteem. This won't be hard for you to do because you'll be excited about her achievements.

> *I praise her to make her feel good. You have to make her feel good so she'll be a good kid.*
>
> *I wasn't brought up like this. I had a pretty rough childhood. My mom was young, and she wasn't around. She left me with my grandparents, and my grandpa would say, "Oh, you're so stupid."*
>
> Miguel, 21 - Genevieve, 18 months (Maurine, 16)

## Emotions Develop Rapidly

Her emotions come through clearly. If there's already a new baby, she probably will be jealous as well as affectionate toward the new sibling.

> *When Sylvia was first born, Crystal didn't like her too well and would hit her. I let her help with the baby and didn't make her feel she was being thrown out. I explained that Sylvia was her baby, too.*
>
> *Now if anybody makes Sylvia cry, Crystal will protect her. When her little cousin hits Sylvia, Crystal hits him.*
>
> Carrie, 18 - Crystal, 31 months; Sylvia, 14 months

She may be wary of strangers, and even of some people she knows. She doesn't like to be picked up too quickly by people she doesn't know well. She's her own person and doesn't want to be grabbed by adults.

> *Alice is real open with most people unless they want to pick her up right away. When she gets used to them, she'll go to them.*
>
> Melanie

## Your Problem-Solving Toddler

*Todd is so busy. I wonder how he got all that
energy. I'll put little crackers in a container, and give
him a second container with it. He'll put the crackers
back and forth from one to the other. You can see how
his little mind works—he'll try to put half on this side
and half on the other.*

*It's unbelievable how much he knows—I guess
more than I really give him credit for.*

Jill, 18 - Todd, 16 months

As Jill said, you can almost see his mind developing.
He's learning more rapidly now than he ever will again.
His world is expanding constantly, and he's trying to keep
up with it.

You might like to research your child's ability to solve a
problem through trial and error. Perhaps she's trying to ride
her kiddie car between two pieces of furniture. She discovers she can't get through, so scoots around the furniture
instead. That's the trial and error method. Something didn't
work, so she tried something else.

## From Bottle or Breast to Cup

If you haven't started encouraging your child to drink
milk, juice, and water from a cup, it's time to do so. Children generally can begin to learn to drink from a cup when
they're about nine months old.

Weaning your child from his bottle or your breast is
likely to go more smoothly if he's had plenty of time to
learn to drink from a cup. Drinking from a cup is quite
different from sucking fluid from a bottle.

The milk enters his mouth faster from a cup, and it
comes into the front of his mouth instead of the back. Not
only will he not be able to suck, he will need to learn how

to hold his lower lip along the edge of the cup. Otherwise, the milk will dribble down his chin.

Many children like to use a cup with a drinking spout. They can still suck a little, and the spout is more like a nipple than is the edge of a cup. Transferring to a cup later won't be especially difficult.

## Weaning— When?

For some children, giving up the bottle is difficult. Some people believe it's easier for the child (and mom and dad) if he switches from his bottle to a cup soon after he's a year old. They feel if he takes his bottle until he's two, for example, he won't want to change—almost like an addiction.

On the other hand, some children appear to need more sucking than others. They suck a thumb or a pacifier for satisfaction. Your child's need to suck will be less as she nears her second birthday. You're the best judge of your child's readiness to give up her bottle.

As you give your baby a bottle of milk, hold her in your lap while you feed her. A child under two will let you know when

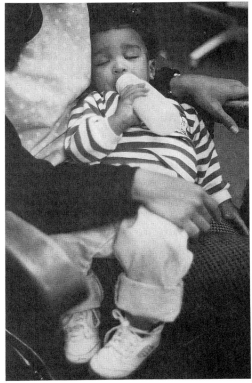

*Hold him while he takes his bottle.*

she's ready to give up the bottle. She will drink a little, then look away or start to play. Two things need to happen at that time:

> • She has to get enough milk—or get enough calcium from another source such as yogurt and cottage cheese.
> • You have to be comfortable that she's telling you she doesn't need the sucking experience any longer.

If your child is hungry at bedtime, give her a light snack or a bottle *before* she goes to bed. Then brush her teeth. If she still needs something to suck on as she drifts off to sleep, give her a bottle of water or a pacifier. Either will satisfy her urge to suck.

There is nothing wrong with going to bed with a bottle—that's just fine. It's a nice comforting thing, and all of us like to be comfortable when we go to bed. But it is not good, whatever your child's age, to have milk in that bottle.

If your child goes to sleep with a bottle of milk in his mouth, the sugar in the milk is likely to cause cavities in his teeth—the Nursing Bottle Syndrome. If your toddler wants a bottle at bedtime, put water in the bottle.

*Alice will take two or three naps during the day. She's attached to her bottle. At night she has to go to sleep with the bottle, but she doesn't care what's in it. I give her water at night. If I give her milk in a cup and water in the bottle, she'll quit demanding the bottle so much.*

Melanie

## Toddlers May Be "At Risk"

Most families probably do a pretty good job of parenting their children during the first six to eight months of life. If they love their babies a lot and respond to their cries for food, warmth, dryness, cuddling, and sleep, their babies will probably do well.

Dr. Burton L. White, parenting seminar leader and author of *The First Three Years of Life* (1990: Prentice Hall), thinks many of us don't do as well as we should with our children during the time they're 8 to 36 months old. He is convinced that a child who doesn't learn as she should before she's three years old may never catch up.

His research shows that children who don't do well in school usually score okay in ability tests until they're a year old. By age two, they're beginning to show problems. By the time they're three years old, they exhibit to quite an extent how well—or how poorly—they will be doing in school a few years later.

---

*Unless you help her, she may not learn to talk as well as she might.*

---

Every child, according to Dr. White, is "at risk" during the period from eight months to two years. She is "at risk" as far as learning as much about her world as she should during this period. Being "at risk" means that, unless her parents and other caregivers provide her with enough learning experiences and plenty of freedom to be curious, she won't learn as she should. She may not be as intelligent as she could have been.

Being "at risk" means the desired behavior/learning will not happen automatically. Unless you help her, she may not talk as well as she might. Unless you guide her in learning to get along with people, her social development won't be as good as it should be. How you respond to her needs today has a great deal to do with the person she becomes.

Your child is an exciting challenge. Your love and your guidance provide the foundation for her future.

*She can put her shoes on now, but sometimes she needs help.*

# She's Struggling for Independence

*Marty hates the word "No." If I say "No," he wants to do the opposite. He's very active. I say anything, and he picks it up, sometimes in sentences.*

*He likes clothes—he likes to put his training pants on and off. He likes hats. He likes dolls. He's even starting to learn to swim.*

Yumiko, 16 - Marty, 21 months

*Derek is kind of bratty now. He'll stick his tongue out at you. He wants to explore, and I let him touch everything. We don't have much out here that he could hurt or that could hurt him.*

Laurette, 17 - Derek, 18 months

The runabout stage in a child's life is one of the most difficult for his parents—and for himself. He's trying to move away from being a dependent baby. So far, he has relied on other people for almost everything. Now he wants to be an independent person who makes many of his own decisions and who is rather self-reliant. To develop properly, he needs to take this step, hard as it is on those around him.

*Infants are okay, but with toddlers, you have to kind of know what you're doing. And you have to take it one day at a time.*

Roseanna, 15 - Felipe, 2

## Toddlers, Like Teenagers, Struggle for Independence

The toddler's "negative stage" has been compared to the beginning of puberty. At that time, as you may remember, young people struggle toward becoming adults who make their own decisions. No longer does the adolescent want her parents to "run her life." A great deal of friction occurs in many families because of the parents' desire to stay in control of their teenager's life while the teenager insists on taking over that control. It's often a difficult time for everyone.

Your toddler probably has similar feelings. No, she doesn't want the family car tonight, but she does want to feel she is in control of what she eats, the clothes she wears, when/whether she uses the bathroom, and how long she plays outside. Giving her the opportunity to make some of these decisions may make it easier for her to comply with your wishes when you can't let her choose.

*Henry is a handful. He doesn't really mess things up and break things, but he climbs, gets into everything. I'm constantly having to watch him while I'm doing everything else. It gets very hectic.*

> *Every time I tell him to do something, he says*
> *"No." Sometimes I put him in the bedroom and shut*
> *the door. He'll bang on the door and cry, and that*
> *gets on my nerves. When I get really uptight, I let*
> *Marvin take care of him, and I get out of the house.*
>
> Olivia, 20 - Henry, 23 months

Teenagers and their parents are ahead if they can each give a little. Perhaps she can't have the family car whenever she wants it, but she can use it for errands and an occasional date. Perhaps she can't stay out as late as she chooses, but maybe she and her parents can arrive at a reasonable compromise.

---

*Your toddler needs to feel she has*
*some control over her life just as you do.*

---

The consequences of treating adolescents either too strictly or too loosely may be severe. They still need parental support, but they also need to be able to take responsibility for their own actions. Teenagers who either lose control of themselves or have never learned to take control of their lives can end up with serious difficulties. They not only may have trouble with other people, but with the law as well.

Parents and toddlers, too, need to adjust to each others' wishes. Your toddler needs to feel she has some control over her life just as you do. A major difference between a teen's struggle for independence and a toddler's struggle is that your toddler can't yet express herself well using words. How would you feel if you had to face the difficulties of adolescence without being able to talk very well? You'd probably feel terribly frustrated.

Compromise and respect are magic ingredients for minimizing the frustrations of living with a toddler. Being sensitive to your child's need to control some aspects of her life will help you to understand her behavior better.

## Temper Tantrums

Temper tantrums happen because of frustration. During this stage, your child will have a lot of negative feelings. He wants so badly to do everything himself. But when he tries to put his clothes on, it's a struggle. Or he tries to put a big can into a little one, and it doesn't work. Yet he doesn't want you to help him.

These and many more happenings add up to a lot of frustration, but he can't talk it out. He doesn't know many words yet so he screams. His screaming may turn into a real out-of-control temper tantrum.

Unlike teenagers, your toddler doesn't have to worry about "outside" law. But losing control—in the form of frequent tantrums—can be pretty frightening for him. He desperately wants to do things his way. At the same time, he needs your firm guidance.

*When Shelly gets really mad, she holds her breath, and I'm afraid she might pass out one of these days. She started when she was ten months old. She turns purple. I blow in her face and she breathes again. Sometimes I scold her. Then I start hugging her because I know she's upset.*

Dixie, 18 - Shelly, 17 months

What should you do?

First, what should you *not* do? Don't spank or otherwise punish your already upset child. If he's having a "real" tantrum, he's lost control of his own actions. If he's "just" screaming, hitting him won't help, and it surely will not stop his screaming.

Don't give in to him either. If he's screaming because you said he couldn't have a piece of candy, don't stop the

screaming by handing over the candy. If you do, what
happens next time he wants candy? You have another
screaming session.

---

*How you respond to his tantrums now
will affect his actions in the future.*

---

Sometimes it's best to ignore a temper tantrum. If you
can't do that because you can't stand the screaming, pick
him up calmly and take him to his room.

An even better approach may be holding him gently.
Feeling the security of your arms may have a calming
effect. After all, he is a very upset little child, and he needs
to know you still love him—even though you won't give in
to his demands.

How you respond to his tantrums now will affect his
actions in the future. If he finds that having a tantrum
means he'll get what he wants, he will act on that learning
and use a tantrum as a technique for getting his own way.

On the other hand, if his parent screams at him, perhaps
hits him to "give him something to cry about," his frustrations will continue to build. He learns that his parents may
not be people he can turn to when he needs help.

He's less likely to become the self confident, problem-
solving, coping individual you'd like him to be. Instead,
he needs to learn better ways of managing his life. You
can help him by staying calm and loving when he has
a tantrum.

See *Teens Parenting—Discipline from Birth to Three* for
a broader discussion of this topic.

## When Your Child Asks for Help

Responding when your child asks for help is the best
way to cut down on the number of tantrums she will have:

- When your child wants you, stop to see what she wants.
- Provide the help she needs if possible.
- Talk briefly at your child's listening level about the event.
- Once you have assisted or comforted and talked to your child, your next step is to leave her alone.

Because of your sensitivity to her needs, your child learns a lot from an interchange like this:

- She learns to use another person (you) as a resource when she can't handle a situation herself.
- She learns that someone thinks her discomfort, excitement, or problem is important, which means *she* is important.
- Her language learning also gets a boost each time this happens.

## "Terrible Twos"?

Often, people speak of the "Terrible Twos" as if extreme negative behavior suddenly turns up after a child's second birthday. For some children, however, this negative attitude starts as early as 13 or 14 months.

At least by the time he is 17 months old, your child will probably enter this difficult phase. He will often want his own way, no matter what. No longer can you distract him by offering a substitute for the forbidden activity. If he sees that you disapprove of whatever he's doing, he may be even more determined to continue doing it. He will often be hard to live with.

Two thoughts may comfort you. First, this happens to just about every child. His negative actions certainly do not mean you are a poor parent or a terrible person. Second, his

*He wants to play with dad's tools.*

extreme negative behavior will probably go away, or at least become much less intense, within a few months. Perhaps by his second birthday, you will find living with him is a little easier.

For many of us, becoming independent is a real struggle from birth to adulthood. When your toddler seems extra difficult, remember that being a toddler is even harder than caring for one. Your toddler needs all the help and respect you can provide.

*If Marty doesn't know how to put something
together, he'll get help. If he wants to read a book, he
brings it to me. He pulls the legs off his plastic doll
and brings them to me. He's pretty independent.
Sometimes if I walk up and try to help him, he seems
to be saying, "Mom, I can do it, leave me alone."*
                                                           Yumiko

You still need to be firm about things that matter, but
give him choices whenever possible. Don't say, "Come to
lunch right this minute." Instead, a few minutes before
lunch is ready, ask, "Do you want to wash your hands for
lunch, or shall I help you?" At bedtime you might say,
"Which book do you want me to read tonight?" During this
negative stage, don't ever say, "Do you want lunch?" or
"Do you want to go to bed?" unless you can handle "No"
for your answer.

Avoid showing your power when possible. Don't order
him to do something unless it's really necessary. If it is
necessary, then of course you insist that he go along with
your wishes.

Routines, not only for bedtime, but also for meals, naps,
baths, and dressing, may help. Let him do it himself as
much as possible. At times, he will insist on doing it himself when you know he can't possibly succeed. He may get
terribly frustrated, but still won't let you help him. You
need far more tact in dealing with a toddler than with the
most temperamental spouse or employer in existence.
Remember—being tactful is simply being sensitive to
another person's feelings.

How much should you help your child? He needs to
continue to be able to call on you as his resource for help
when he needs it. Sometimes a child of this age seems not
to want to work things out for himself. If he always wants
mother to help him put the puzzle together, either it's too

hard for him, or he isn't learning to be as independent as he should be.

Use your best judgement. Help him when you think he needs you—if he wants you to or will let you. Guide him toward more independence when you think this is advisable.

## Her Skills Increase Rapidly

By your child's second birthday, she may be able to pedal a small tricycle. If she has had practice, she can walk down stairs alone, but she still needs to hang on to the stair railing.

Your almost-two-year-old may be running more than she walks. She can walk on low walls if you hold one of her hands. She can even walk a few steps on tiptoe if you show her how.

By this age, she can take off her clothes, and even put most of them back on. It helps if you choose easy-to-put-on clothing. In fact, when you're shopping for her and looking at items, consider the ease with which she can help dress herself. Easy-to-put-on clothes can save her—and you—a lot of frustration.

If you choose clothes with big buttons or zippers and shoes with velcro fasteners, you'll make it easier for her. Wide sleeves with big armholes and wide-necked garments will also help.

## Coping with Fears

If your child is afraid of the noise of trains and trucks, toilet flushing, police sirens, or the vacuum cleaner, be patient with her.

She may have other fears. Whatever they are, they are real to her. Telling her it's "nothing to be afraid of" won't help her cope. Accept the fears for the realities they are.

Gently help her cope. If she's afraid of the dark, for example, provide a little night light. If she's fearful of storms, let her stay close to you until it's over. If you're not afraid, she probably will follow your example eventually.

## Don't Rush Toilet-Training

Toilet training is not an appropriate task for most children under two. They simply are not ready. Efforts spent at toilet training a child too soon result mostly in frustration for parents and child.

For a discussion of toilet training, see chapter 9 in this book. For a broader coverage, see *Teens Parenting— Discipline from Birth to Three*.

## Major Tasks for Parents

As a parent of a child just learning to get around, you have three major tasks. First, you need to design your child's world so that she can satisfy her curiosity without getting hurt and without causing damage to your home. If you can child-proof your house or apartment and your yard, you'll be doing your child and yourself a favor.

Your second job is to react to your child when she wants you. She may want your help because she's frustrated at something she can't do herself. She may have hurt herself slightly and needs comforting. Or she may be excited and want you to share her excitement. Your assistance, comfort, and enthusiasm are important to her.

It's crucial to your child's learning that you respond promptly to her needs and to her interests. If you're talking on the phone, it's better to say, "I'm talking on the phone. I'll be with you in a minute," than it is to ignore her. Of course, you'll then need to be with her "in a minute."

Your third major responsibility with your child is to carry out your role as authority. Being firm is often necessary. Don't say "No" constantly, or you'll destroy some of your child's curiosity. When you do say "No," mean what you say.

If you say "No," then you laugh because she looks pretty funny sitting in the middle of the dining table playing in the sugar bowl, is she going to take you seriously? Instead, say "No," get her down from the table, and put the sugar bowl away.

The important thing is to see that she carries out your requests. At this age, this generally means removing your child from the situation or distracting her. Ideally, you won't say "No" a second time because you'll already have taken care of the problem.

## Most Important Stage in Life

Helping your toddler develop well is perhaps the greatest challenge you will ever face. How she develops socially and intellectually now is the basis for all of her future development in these areas. Her growth in language and curiosity during this time is of vital importance.

> *Marty explores everything. He opens doors, closets, drawers, pulls all his clothes out. I just go in there and pick them up and make him help.*
>
> *It's not that drastic when a kid pulls his clothes out of his drawer. When he's old enough, he'll fold them up himself. Now he helps. . . he hands them to me.*
>
> Yumiko

While parenting during this stage has many difficult times, you will also find lots of enjoyment in a well-developing toddler. You will find you're no longer living with a baby but, rather, with a young and very interesting little person.

*Enjoy your child!*

*She likes to wash her dolls when mom bathes the baby.*

# Active Play—
# A Toddler's Work

*What I like about her is she's fun. She's real playful with almost everybody. You play with her just a little bit and she'll smile a lot. She always has a smile on her face. People say she looks like me. I like taking her with me to the park when I go there with my friends to play handball.*

Kyle, 16 - Liliane, 15 months

*Meghan likes to figure things out. She loves things that are not toys, especially her father's tools and hammers. Of course she only plays with them when daddy is right beside her.*

*She loves to play with keys, to unlock the doors like mommy and daddy. She likes to play outside with the kids, but she still comes in often to check on me.*

*When I take her to the park, she climbs. At first,
she wanted me to come get her down from each thing,
but I thought she should learn a little independence. I
would sort of close my eyes and not help her for
awhile. It seemed mean, but I thought if I'm there to
do it, she'll expect mommy to help her all the time.
She's very independent.*

Louise, 19 - Meghan, 23 months; Mark, 5 months

Playing with your child is important. He loves to play
with you. As you play, stop occasionally to watch him
without interrupting his play. You can learn a lot about the
ways he likes to play.

Let him lead you into playing at his level. Building
elaborate block structures while he watches is not exactly
playing *with* him. He won't learn as much if he simply
watches you as he will if he's actively playing.

During this time he will start holding things in both
hands. He'll stack blocks on top of each other. Emptying
and filling containers may keep him entertained for a
considerable time.

As his language develops, ask him to talk about his play.
What is he doing? If he's scribbling or coloring, ask him
about his picture. Don't say, "What is that?" Instead,
suggest, "Tell me about your drawing."

Remember that his attention span is still very short.
When he decides to stop playing, respect his judgment.

## Active Play Is Valuable

Running, climbing, jumping, swinging, and generally
leaping about are all important for your toddler's development. Playground equipment can be exciting for her if it's
not too large or elaborate and hard to use. If she can climb
it herself—and if she wants to— she's probably safe. Don't
help her much, and don't urge her to play on something

about which she feels fearful. Sometimes you may need to help her get down.

Toddlers generally love to swing. Do you have a tree or something else to use for hanging a swing? An old tire on a strong rope makes a great swing.

Some toddlers would rather be pushed in the swing than do almost anything else.

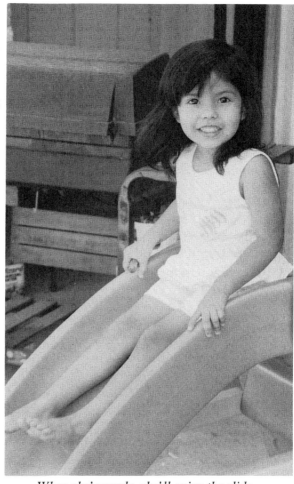

*When she's ready, she'll enjoy the slide.*

If you have your own house, you might put a couple of strong hooks in the joists or rafters above a play space. Securely tie a thick soft rope to the hooks. Put a big knot at the other end. Your child can hold on to it and try to straddle it. Later, when she's older, you might even put a rope ladder on it for her. This could be a good project for grandpa.

Acrobatics are fun for toddlers. Is there any way you can let her play on an old crib mattress on the floor? Jumping on your bed can be pretty destructive even if you remove the bedspread and your child takes her shoes off. If you have an old mattress or foam rubber pad you can put on the floor, she'll love playing on it.

> *Shelly is very active. She'll watch people do something, then try to copy them. My cousin does gymnastics, and she tries to do what he does.*
>
> Dixie, 18 - Shelly, 17 months

If you don't have stairs in your home, find some occasionally so she can practice going up and down. Otherwise, she's apt to fall when she's at the top of a flight of stairs with no practice in coming down safely.

> *Shelly is good at stairs now. She used to fall. She climbs them on her knees, then comes down on her butt. At first, it was a problem. When she was real quiet, I'd know she was going upstairs. I let her go, but I was right behind her.*
>
> Dixie

A board about eight inches wide and six feet long makes a good "toy." Your toddler can use it for a balancing board. Putting one foot directly in front of the other is a hard task for toddlers. She can practice on the board. She can also practice this skill on the lines of your floor tiles.

Walking the plank is even more fun if you set it up on two low piles of magazines. An inch above the floor is plenty high at first. Later, your child will be able to walk up when one end is raised slightly.

She'll enjoy riding toys although she may not be ready for a tricycle until she's at least two. Best is a low kiddie car in which she can sit and push herself along with her feet. You need to look for one that is simply built and won't spread her legs too far apart. Remember that toddlers have short legs. Some plastic cars are built too wide.

Competent as your toddler is, you still need *always* to supervise water play, whether in the bathtub or outdoors. She will continue to enjoy this kind of play, especially if you join her. She may even be able to blow soap bubbles soon.

Remember, however, that a child can drown in an inch of water. She should *never* be left alone with even a little water in the tub or play pool.

## Play Ball!

Sometime after her first birthday, she will enjoy throwing things. She has learned how to let go of items, and will enjoy simple ball games in which she can toss the ball.

By the time she's two, she may be able to throw overhand more or less in your direction. She can kick a ball, too. Sometimes the dog joins the game:

> *We play ball. I throw the ball, the dog picks it up and brings it to me, puts it down. Todd then picks it up and throws it.*
>
> *We always play chase in the house. I act like I'm a monster and I'm going to get him. He loves it.*
>
> Jill, 18 - Todd, 16 months

> *Sean throws a big ball and kicks it. He's been playing with it for about two weeks. He has a smaller one that he throws around and kicks, too.*
>
> Ginger, 18 - Sean, 17 months

A tennis ball can provide a lot of fun for a toddler. She can have a wonderful time throwing it and watching it bounce. It's easier for her to handle than is a bigger ball.

Perhaps best of all, she's less likely to knock a lamp over, put out a window, or hurt another child with a tennis ball.

*She picks up everything. She tries to play baseball. She'll hit it and do the running. She always slides into base. She's a real character.*

Darla, 17 - Janis, 2

## Play Space, Play Time Needed

Wherever you live, even if it's a crowded apartment, try to make play space for your toddler. It's still best if this space can be part of the kitchen or living room close to you rather than in a room away from everyone.

Organizing your child's play materials is important. If he can't find part of the toy he wants, he won't play well. Does he seem to have lots of toys that he doesn't use? Are some of them broken? Are there parts missing? Are they hard to find at the bottom of a deep toy box? Are they hidden behind storage doors?

Perhaps you can get a few open shelves. Cement blocks and boards, if not stacked too high, make good shelving. Make sure they are stable so your toddler can't push them down. Help him keep his big toys on the bottom shelf, his others where he can reach them.

It's wise to have only a few toys readily available, the toys he's really interested in at the time. When you bring his other toys out again, they may seem new and interesting. Besides, if you leave everything out, a child this age will simply throw them all over the floor. You may even want him to use the more complicated stacking toys only at times when you can play with him.

Roseanna, 15, and Felipe, 2, lived in a small apartment with little storage space. Roseanna placed several hooks high on the wall. On each hook she hung a pillowcase of toys. They came down for play one at a time.

The apartment was less of a disaster area, and Felipe's play undoubtedly was more satisfying to him. He wasn't confused by seeing all his toys dumped out at once.

## Play With Him Often

*I love this age when Derek is running around. It makes me feel good that I can teach him something. After dinner he starts winding up again, so I usually take him for a walk. He wants to know what everything is. By the time we get back, he's pretty calm again.*

Laurette, 17 - Derek, 18 months

Laurette is a wise mother. Taking Derek for a walk when he's "wound up" is much better for both of them than would an attempt by his mother to insist he "Calm down right now!" In addition, chances are good that Derek will be ready for bed after he's had his walk with his mom.

Play with your child regularly. Hopefully, you'll do this because you want to. Of course your work and activities take a lot of time, and they—and you—are very important. But if he has to whine and beg to get your attention, the ten minutes of play you finally give him won't be much fun for either of you.

Make the most of whatever time you can give your child. Be sure to give him your full attention. Follow his lead— does he want to roll a ball back and forth? Then play ball with him.

Tomorrow he may decide to let you help him build a tower with his blocks, or perhaps he'll be ready to fingerpaint. Always talk to him about whatever you're doing together.

A follow-the-leader game is easy to organize right in your living room. You be the leader first, and crawl under the table, around a chair, through a big box you've placed

there, and over the big ball beside the box. Next time, let
your child be the leader.

## Bowling Game

Use two-quart milk cartons for the bowling pins. You
may need to put blocks inside them to give them enough
stability to stand up. Then show your youngster how to
roll a ball toward the "pins" to try to knock them over.

Throwing newspaper balls is fun for a toddler and
remarkably safe for your house. Crumple newspaper into a
ball and hold it together with a little tape. Make several and
offer them to your child.

If he's naming small objects such as a ball, a car, a
spoon, and a doll, make him a feel-box. A box in which
small appliances are shipped is usually sturdy enough for
this game. Cut a hole in the side big enough for your
child's hand.

Show him the little items one at a time. Let him handle
and examine them. Then put each one inside the box. Ask
him to put his hand in the box and pick up an item. Then,
without taking it out or looking at it, ask him to tell you
what it is.

## Classifying Objects

You may notice your toddler is beginning to sort items
into groups. This is a start toward making sense out of his
world by classifying things and people into categories. He
has already classified people into those he knows and trusts
and those he doesn't. He certainly classifies toys into
"mine" and, more slowly, "yours."

When you purchase toys for him, a good set of small
objects is a good buy. Be sure none of the parts are so small
that he could choke on them. Perhaps you'll choose a city

street scene or a barn with animals and people. You'll find he begins playing by classifying—dividing the people from the animals, for example.

Soon he will be creating scenes and using his imagination. He'll make the cars go fast, the dogs chase one another, and the policemen stop traffic.

## Plan for Indoor Play

Scribbling has been called the art of the toddler. Scribbling is how she learns to draw. Instead of teaching her to draw later, show her how to scribble

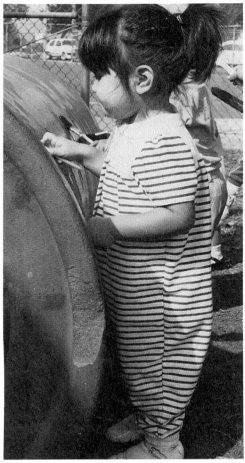

*Painting outside means less mess inside.*

during her second year. Her scribbling will turn into drawing a year or so from now.

Putting out big sheets of paper for painting and scribbling is important. You don't have to buy paper. Just put in front of your child big paper bags that have been cut open. First, you put a mark on the paper with an oversized kindergarten crayon. Then hand the crayon to her saying, "Now you color." She will love it.

She will also need supervision unless you want the scribbling extended to your walls, furniture, and telephone book. For more about this, see *Teens Parenting—Discipline from Birth to Three*.

It's time to make or buy a few simple puzzles for your child. Paste a picture on cardboard, then cut it in three pieces. Can she fit them together? If she does it quickly, perhaps she's ready for a harder task. If so, cut the same puzzle into five or six pieces. Can she still put it together?

She can probably place a circle and a square in a formboard. You can make one for her by drawing a big square and circle on a piece of cardboard. Cut out the same size square and circle from white paper. Color the shapes to match those on the cardboard. Can she match them yet?

Another "game" idea—suggest she sort the laundry or her clothes by color.

## Toys from Home

You can make a stacking toy for your child using empty food containers. Use various sizes of cans such as juice, tomato paste, and soup cans. Be sure to go around each can a second time with a can opener. Then feel each one to see if any sharp edges remain. If it's still sharp, throw it away and try another can.

Your child will like the designs on the cans, but if you want something fancier, cover them with glued-on fabric. Putting fur on one, silk on another, and vinyl on the third adds nice touching experience to the stacking game.

She may be able to string large "beads" now. The beads can be empty spools, empty tape rollers, or even hair rollers. Dip about two inches of the end of some cord in white glue. Let it dry, and it will be stiff enough for your toddler to stick it through the holes. The cord should be no longer than ten inches. You don't want to run the risk of her wrapping the cord around her neck.

A few months ago, your child probably learned to stack one block on top of another. Now she can make a higher stack, a tower of blocks. Or she may stack cans of food, one on top of the other.

*Lance climbs right into the cupboards with the pots and pans. Then he puts them inside each other. He can play in the lower cupboards although I rubberbanded one that I don't want him into.*

Celia, 21 - Laurel, 4; Lance, 18 months

She will enjoy rearranging all kinds of objects around the house. She may take everything out of your kitchen cupboard and line the items up on the floor. She may balk at putting them away. If the job seems too much for her, ask her to help you put them back.

Perhaps she'd like to sort them by color or size. Then you'd say, "Let's put all the big ones away first." Or make a game of seeing if she can put them away as fast as you put lunch on the table.

*Sean explores a lot. He gets into cupboards, everything you let him get into. He gets out the pans and bangs them together. He also bangs the cupboard doors back and forth.*

Ginger

Play is your child's work. Through play, she learns more about her world. Joining in her play is an important part of building a good relationship with her. Time spent playing with her is likely to mean less time spent solving problems she causes because of boredom or lack of attention.

Most important, you and your toddler can enjoy each other tremendously!

*She has a marvelous time pretending.*

# Her Imagination Soars

*Leon pretends he's a dog, a cat, a bird flying. Sometimes he rides a horse (on the arm of the couch). He and DeeDee will go in the bedroom and pretend they're in outer space. They will sit and talk and talk. He understands her and she understands him.*

Tamara, 21 - DeeDee, 4; Leon, 20 months

Often children in this age group have a marvelous time pretending. They love to dress up in mother's or daddy's clothes. Putting on your shoes may be a favorite activity for him. Different kinds of hats will fascinate him. Save some of your old clothes for his dress-up play.

*Antonio plays house with his cowboys, soldiers, and boats. He loves motorcycles—the little ones and the real ones. We went by the shop yesterday, and he wanted to get on one.*

*He will tell his doll "No" which is what I tell him.*
*Or he'll say, "Behave yourself."*

Becky, 18 - Antonio, 26 months

Soon your child may involve you in her make-believe
play. If she invites you to feed her teddy bear, do so. Your
participation is good for her, and besides, you'll have
fun, too.

*Janis does a lot of acting. I got sample diapers in*
*the mail the other day. She went in and got them and*
*said, "These are for me. The mailman sent them*
*for me." She asked me to put them on her, so I did.*
*Then she pretended she was a baby and crawled*
*around.*
*She likes music a lot, punk rock. She sees my*
*brother pretend like he's playing a guitar, so she does*
*it, too.*

Darla, 17 - Janis

Dolls are important to almost all children. Most parents
now seem to understand boys need dolls as much as girls
do. After all, if playing with dolls is early practice toward
being a parent, it must be as important for boys as for girls.
Most men, as well as most women, will become parents.

*Janet has two dolls, a boy doll and a bear doll,*
*Frankie and Henry. She takes them in the tub with*
*her. She calls them her babies and takes them to bed.*

Candi, 16 - Janet, 18 months

Most toddlers love music. She may turn the radio on so
she'll have music for her dancing. Dance with her if she
asks you. You'll both enjoy it.

She'd like her own musical instrument such as a drum,
cymbals, or musical triangle. You can make her a drum
from a one-pound coffee can. Two pan lids make cymbals.

Toddlers love bells. You have to supervise two or more toddlers ringing bells because in their exuberance they might hit each other. It's worth the effort, however.

## Let Him "Help"

*Henry will open the drawer and get a can opener. Then he'll get a can and give it to me, or he'll try to open the can himself. He likes to do what I do. He can even unlock the front door himself.*

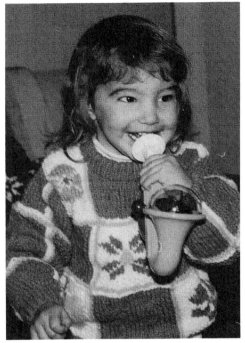

*Today she's a musician.*

Olivia, 20 - Henry, 23 months

Toddlers generally love to "help" with the housework. If he can have a small broom, he'll sweep right along with you. Mopping the floor with a rag is his idea of real play.

When you're cooking, you can think of ways to involve him. Let him add the seasonings—pre-measured by you, of course. If you're baking, he can sift ingredients and help you stir the mixture.

If you can figure a way to let him help you wash dishes without having a nervous breakdown yourself, he'll love it. If you have two sinks, he can use one to wash plastic spoons, cups, plates, and pans. You'll probably be ahead if you put a lot of newspapers on the floor before he starts washing dishes. Then his spills can be rolled up and thrown away. Or put bath towels on the floor to catch the water.

He can be a real help at times. He can follow your simple request, "Bring me the dustcloth." He can help you make the beds, especially his own. He will love to mimic you.

## Toddlers and Talking

You've been helping your child learn to speak ever since she was born. You've talked to her, named things and people, read to her. She may be saying quite a few words by now.

*Felipe talks quite a bit. He says names, "Rock-a-bye baby," "Book," a lot of things.*

Roseanna, 15 - Felipe, 2

*Sean knows his body parts—nose, eyes, mouth, ears, hands, feet, legs. He just learned his arms yesterday. He answers the telephone. He says, "Who's this?" and then keeps talking.*

Ginger, 18 - Sean, 17 months

*Todd is starting to say two words together—"Go bye-bye."*

Jill, 18 - Todd, 16 months

If there are words you don't want your toddler to learn, try not to have those words said when she's around. She's learning to talk by repeating the words she hears. Punishing a child for using "bad" words doesn't make much sense. To the child, all the words she hears are interesting, and she should not be expected to censor her own speech for several years.

An infant center teacher talked about a two-year-old whose language was outrageous. "We didn't make a big deal of it," she reported. "We ignored the word. We went on as if he didn't say it. We would distract him to something else. Sometimes we'd comment in a matter-of-fact way, 'Oh, we don't use that word.' Then we'd go on to another activity. Gradually his language improved."

## Don't Correct His Speech

Now that he's beginning to say a few words, there are two more ways you can help him.

First, don't correct his speech. When you talk to him, pronounce the words correctly and clearly. But if he says "pitty" for "pretty," don't worry about it. He'll learn faster if you don't criticize.

Second, your child may not bother talking if he sees no need to do so. If he points at the refrigerator, do you immediately hand him a cup of juice? If he gestures for a

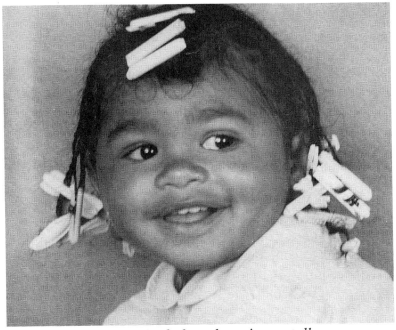

*She's excited about learning to talk.*

cracker, do you give it to him right now? Instead, try encouraging him to say the word when possible. Don't frustrate him, of course, by waiting more than a few seconds. Remember that children start talking at different ages.

> *Shelly pulls at me to get attention. She says "Bottle" and "Eat." If she wants something, she calls it out. She's been doing that for about two months.*
>
> Dixie, 18 - Shelly, 17 months

> *Marty sits there jabbering. He sounds like he knows what he's talking about, but I can't understand what he's saying.*
>
> Yumiko, 16 - Marty, 21 months

While most children can name familiar things and occasionally speak in two-word phrases toward the end of the second year, your perfectly bright two-year-old may say scarcely a word. Don't worry about it. Continue talking to him about the things you're doing with him. Use simple, clear, slow speech.

By the end of this stage, your child may be talking in "sentences." His version of a sentence, however, is generally one word such as "Hi." If he says "Up," he means "Pick me up." Don't expect sentences complete with a noun, a verb, and an object. Most children don't speak in real sentences until after their second birthday.

## Book of (his name)'s Words

Use light cardboard for the pages. The cardboard in panty hose packages works well. Punch holes in the pages and tie them together with yarn. Find pictures to represent the words he's saying. "Ma-ma," "Da-da," "Bye," and "Dog" may be his first understandable words. Put a picture of each in the book, then read it with him. Soon he may be "reading" the pictures to you.

# Read to Your Child

If you've been reading to your child, he's probably talking more than he would have otherwise.

*I read to Shelly. I think that helps her learn to talk. I started reading to her when she was ten months old.*

*I don't like to read unless it's what I want to read. But when I read to Shelly, I know what I'm getting out of it. I enjoy it. And she starts mumbling as though she's reading. That's how she learned the names of doggie, etc. She turns the pages herself.*

Dixie

*Sean takes a book, opens it up, and jabbers like he's reading. I read to him a lot. He likes to point at the pictures, and he listens when I read to him.*

Ginger

The pictures are the important thing. Don't get hung up on teaching your child to read for several years yet. You can count on him learning to read with less struggle later if he enjoys books with you now.

When you choose books for your toddler, you'll want those with bright, simple pictures. At this age, her favorites will probably be books with pictures of things and people she already knows about.

*Heidi loves picture books. I read to her. She has books in her toy box. She looks at them, then shows me and grunts that she wants me to read to her. It's really amazing how she wants to talk so bad.*

Jenny, 18 - Heidi, 13 months

If her grandparents live with or near you, a book about a child playing with Gramps will interest her. Books about dogs and cats are good. She may especially like stories with pictures of babies.

As she grows older, of course, you won't limit her books to stories about familiar things. The rhythm of Mother Goose rhymes will appeal to her. Fairy tales and stories about animals, people, and places she has never seen are an important part of her education. Provide lots of variety in her books, because books can widen her knowledge of and interest in many different things. Books about familiar topics, however, are more likely to keep a toddler's interest.

## Choose Non-Sexist Books

Books can play an important part in a child's learning about himself and his world. Don't let his books show a

slanted, sexist picture of the world. Too often, children's picture books portray all mothers in the kitchen cooking dinner and all fathers out earning the living.

Children's picture books sometimes suggest through illustrations and words that little girls stay clean, play quietly, and cry occasionally. Little boys, however, are expected to play roughly and get dirty, but aren't supposed to cry.

*Reading with mom is a special time.*

A horrible example of such a book, *I'm Glad I'm a Boy, I'm Glad I'm a Girl,* was published in 1970 by Simon and Schuster. It included such statements as "Boys have trucks. Girls have dolls. Boys are doctors. Girls are nurses. Boys invent things. Girls use what boys invent. Boys are policemen. Girls are metermaids."

This book is, fortunately, out of print. Books still on the market, however, may carry a similar message. They may indicate you can do some things and not others simply because you are a boy or you are a girl.

Look for books that show boys and girls, men and women, as human beings with lots of different abilities and interests. Don't choose stories and illustrations that suggest that your child must limit his/her interests because of his/her sex.

You want your daughter to be glad she's a girl. You want your son to be glad he's a boy. But an athlete, a doctor, or a police officer can be glad she's a woman. A nurse, a dancer, or a preschool teacher can be glad he's a man. Books can help your child realize the wonderful opportunities open to boys and girls, to men and to women. Choose those books carefully.

As you read to your child and encourage the development of her imagination, you're laying the foundation for successful school experiences for him later. In fact, you are your child's most important teacher. He will learn far more interacting with you during this stage than he ever will again.

*You have a wonderful challenge!*

*Both dad and toddler win if dad's involved.*

# CHAPTER 5

# Dad's Ahead
# If He's Involved

*A lot of fathers don't live with their kid. They just come in and visit on weekends or after school while I can see Alex all the time. I saw him when he started walking, and when he first said "Daddy." That makes me more involved with him.*

*Alex made me less selfish in a way that I just can't go out and get everything for me. I have to consider that he needs this, he gets that. I have a lot to share with him. Like now I'm trying to teach him to catch a ball. I'm like every other father in wanting him to be a baseball star, and I want to get him out there young.*

*I didn't expect to have a baby this young. I hadn't planned on it until I was 25 when I would be stable and set and it was time to have kids. It just happened.*

Brian, 20 - Alex, 12 months (Erin, 16)

Teen mothers or fathers who parent alone often have to learn how to take complete responsibility for caring for their child(ren). Most of the time it's the teen mother who cares for the child if the parents aren't together. No matter how tired she is, she's the one who feeds him, plays with him, takes care of him when he's sick, and performs all the other parenting tasks because she's the live-in parent.

## Some Fathers Are Very Involved

Ideally, if the parents live together, they share childcare responsibilities. If dad is not the baby's biological father, he may still play that role. While it's important to be honest with your child concerning his biological father, the man who actually parents him may be someone else.

More and more fathers are realizing how much better their relationship with their child is if they're deeply involved in caring for that child. They know that if only mom takes care of the baby, dad misses out:

*I'm as involved in Dustin's life as Kelly Ellen is. We both share everything with him. I've felt real attached since the moment he was born.*

*I change him, feed him and bathe him, cut his nails, everything. We both read to him. Books are his favorite now. Everywhere we go he's got to have books. He has his favorites.*

*In sports, you learn everything you can to be the best you can be. I feel that way about him. I want him to be brought up the best way we can. Every day is a different day with him. Every day we learn something, whether it's his personality change or something we learn from another child in another family.*

*I take care of Dustin because I love him. If I didn't love him, I wouldn't be here. He's part of me, and I want to be with him and bring him up.*

Mark, 22 - Dustin, 30 months (Kelly Ellen, 20)

Sometimes dad is not the child's biological father. If you're with someone else, someone who plays the father role, you may already know the "real" dad is the one who loves the child and takes daily responsibility for him.

If your partner is not your child's father, how involved should he be in childcare? That depends on a lot of things. If you're developing a strong relationship and you expect to be together for a long time, he will probably want to be quite involved with your child.

> *Teri's real close to Greg. Even though he isn't her natural father, he's her father. Like when I was pregnant, he would get up in the middle of the night when she needed him. He's the one who picks her up from school. That's a father, someone who is there for her, who feeds her and bathes her, not someone who made her.*
>
> Carla, 21 - Teri, 5; Manuel, 14 months

It's always best to be honest with your toddler. Even if she never sees her father, she needs to know she has another dad.

## Others Leave It Up to Mom

Dads do indeed play an important role in a child's life. Some fathers, however, even if they live with their children, leave the childcare up to mom.

> *Dennis isn't too much help, perhaps because of the problems we've had. He thinks the baby is just mine. His mom helps me a lot, and my mom did when I lived at home. You can get very irritable if you don't have anybody to help you.*
>
> Jenny, 18 - Heidi, 13 months

Louise expressed that irritability forcefully:

*Bob isn't always here, and when he is, he isn't that much help. Last night I blew up at him. When he gets home, I like to sit down and relax. So I went next door to visit a friend.*

*As soon as one of the kids says "Boo," he comes over and gets me. I asked him, "Can't I ever leave this house to take a break without having you coming after me, or Meghan tagging along?"*

*If he goes out that door to visit some of the guys in the complex here, I'm not to bother him. It seems like mother is supposed to do everything with the kids.*

Louise, 19 - Mark, 5 months; Meghan, 23 months

Mick didn't expect to change his daughter's diapers and feed her, perhaps because he didn't live with her until she was 14 months old. In fact, Kris continued doing these tasks for several months after they moved in with Mick and his family. Then Kris got a weekend job, and Mick discovered he had no choice:

*When Kris and Cassandra moved in with us, I didn't think I'd be taking care of Cassie. Then Kris started working weekends, so I have Cassie all day Saturday and Sunday.*

*At first I'd say, "Mom, change her diaper." She would say, "No, you do it."*

*Or I'd tell my sisters to change her. "No, it's your kid," they would tell me. I had no choice.*

*Now I feed her and play with her a lot. We play basketball. I take her to the park and we play kickball.*

Mick, 19 - Cassandra, 25 months (Kris, 17)

## Building a Family

If you're the dad, how much time do you spend with your child? Do you do your share of diaper changing and

*Dad's shoulder—his favorite spot in the whole world.*

bath-giving? Do you play with him now, or are you waiting until he's big enough to play football with you?

If you're the mother, do you assume you should be the one to be with your toddler most of the time? Or would you like dad, if he's with you, to get more involved?

Ernesta felt very strongly that mother and father should share childcare. She understood the benefits not only to herself, but for the baby and the father. Osvaldo didn't agree at first, but Ernesta didn't give up her dream of a family with both parents involved with their children:

> *At first when the baby needed changing, my husband would say, "No, that's the mother's job."*
>
> *I'd say, "No, it's not just the mother's job. I didn't have the baby by myself. It took both of us."*
>
> *In the beginning he wouldn't help. We fought a lot about that. Finally I told his mom that he didn't want to help me do anything. His mom got mad at him and told him, "You have to help her."*

*My father never helped my mom, so I grew up
without any idea of how to talk to my dad. I told
Osvaldo, "If you want a relationship like that, forget
it. We'll just end our relationship right here. I want a
family where the father is very involved." That made
him think about it.*

---

There's mother/father love,
not just mother love for the baby.

---

*We even went to see a counselor once, and she
helped us a lot.*

*Now he helps me, and I think it's great. I think all
fathers should, not just because mothers need help,
but because he has to build a relationship with the
baby himself. There's mother/father love, not just
mother love for the baby.*

Ernesta, 20 - Jeremy, 3; Osvaldo, Jr., 5 months

Osvaldo undoubtedly has a better relationship with his
children because of Ernesta's insistence that he share in the
childcare.

## Learning to Be a Father

Meghan, too, was convinced that parenting is for mothers *and* fathers. Her father was never at home as she was
growing up.

Tim's parents played the traditional roles of dad out
working and mom home with the kids. Meghan wanted
more for their children.

She and Tim didn't marry until Angel was nearly two. In
fact, they split up during pregnancy, and Tim didn't see his
son until Angel was five months old. From that time on, he
spent a lot of time with Meghan and Angel. Meghan shared
their story:

*I said Tim didn't need to be with me but I wanted
our son to know him. He started coming over, and he
started playing daddy real quick. I showed him how
to change diapers. I said, "You need to be part of his
life. I'll show you how to change a diaper. You'll
catch on, you will."*

*He was scared. He didn't know how to take care of
Angel. He would always ask me what to do, and I
said, "You're his father. You have to learn these
things."*

---

## Maybe your father didn't give you a bath, does that mean you can't bathe Angel?

---

*Once when Angel needed a bath, and I told Tim to
do it, he said "No."*

*I said, "Why not?"*

*"My father never gave me a bath."*

*I asked him to leave. He got me upset, and I didn't
want to be upset in front of Angel because I knew a
baby gets upset if you're upset. Tim asked why I
wanted him to leave.*

*I said, "You're his father and I'm his mother, and I
thought we were in this 50-50. These are not the old
days. Maybe your father didn't give you a bath, does
that mean you can't bathe Angel? This is a whole
different situation. Maybe you had a bad childhood,
but don't take it out on Angel."*

*He looked at me and said, "You're right again."*

*I said, "Don't be scared. I'll be there to help you.
Nothing can happen except get him clean."*

*So we worked past that one and he started giving
Angel baths. Then he started doing just about everything. His family has the old traditions. The mother is*

*in the kitchen and she's pregnant. She takes care of*
*the kids and daddy doesn't do anything with the kids.*
*They kind of resented that I got Tim to change.*

*We agreed that whatever we do is our business.*
*We're a family now, so whatever they think, they can*
*keep their opinions to themselves.*

Meghan, 25 - Angel, 8; Kenny, 6; Jose, 2; Leon, 8 months

Keeping up with a superactive toddler is hard. As
Meghan understood so well, if two parents can share the
childcare, everyone will be better off. Mother won't get so
exhausted, daddy will enjoy his child more if he's involved,
and baby, of course, will be most pleased of all.

## When Dad Lives Elsewhere

Some couples stay together throughout pregnancy, but
don't get married. Many break up after the baby is born. In
fact, the majority of teenage parents, whether or not they
marry, are not together by the time their child is three, or
even two years old.

Many, like Yumiko and Marc, never live together.
During the early months of parenting, the couple may see a
great deal of each other, but their relationship eventually
ends. Where does dad fit in at this point?

Yumiko and Marc attended different high schools. Marc
was working, but he saw Yumiko nearly every day during
her pregnancy. For another year they remained close. He
spent most evenings with Yumiko and Marty.

As the months went by, Yumiko, 15, realized she was
growing up faster than Marc. They started fighting and
finally split. Yumiko is seeing another man now. She
described Marc's relationship with Marty:

*Marc doesn't take much responsibility for Marty. I*
*used to push him when we were together. I'd say,*
*"You're a father now. You should do this."*

*Now he doesn't come to see him very often. Several times he's called and said he was coming over to take Marty somewhere, and then he doesn't show up. That was disappointing for Marty. I don't feel there is any big reason for Marty to go over there. I don't think it hurts him, but he doesn't need it.*

*I think Marc feels he doesn't have to worry about seeing Marty because he'll always have some legal rights. I don't like the idea of him showing up when Marty is five and saying, "Hello, I'm your daddy." I think it's unfair to a kid for daddy to show up just when he feels like it.*

*Sometimes I feel like saying, "Go do your own thing, Marc. Don't even come over here." I can't do that, but I would think he could stop by here at least once a week. Marty was used to seeing him every day. He calls Marc "Daddy," but he doesn't really know what that means.*

Yumiko, 16 - Marty, 21 months

Marc is losing out the most in this situation. He's not building a good relationship with Marty. In fact, it won't be a relationship at all if he continues ignoring his little boy.

## Maintaining a Relationship

Many fathers who don't live with their children want a strong relationship with them. Kyle is an example:

*Last night when Dorene came over, I was going out. All my friends were outside waiting for me, and here comes the mom with the baby. So I told my friends to go on because I was going to stay with my baby.*

*At first I was disappointed because I wanted to go out with my friends. Then Liliane ran toward me*

*smiling, and I knew I wanted to stay with her. My
baby comes first, although sometimes it's hard.*
                    Kyle, 16 - Liliane, 15 months (Dorene, 16)

Miguel lived with his daughter's mother for several
months after Genevieve was born. In fact, if he had his
way, he would still be living with his family. Since that's
not possible, he spends as much time with Genevieve as he
can:

*I'll continue to keep Genevieve whenever I can and
buy her things she needs. If I go shopping, it's not me
I have on my mind, it's them, and I'll buy them
something.*

*Today I didn't go to work so I kept Genny all day.
She's not only my daughter—she's like a little friend.
I was playing with her all day. She's all active—she
gets me tired, but I love her so much I'd do anything
for her.*

*She goes in all the rooms and I have to be alert.
She's smart. She does things I wouldn't think she
would do. I'll tell her to go get me a diaper. She'll do
it, and I'll give her a hug. Every time she does
something good, I hug her.*
                    Miguel, 20 - Genevieve, 18 months (Maurine, 16)

Miguel also talked about the changes he has made in his
life because of his daughter:

*Maurine, Genny, and I lived together about six
months. It was good. I worked long hours, and then I
would see her. Sometimes I even worked on weekends, but when I didn't, I spent all my time with her.*

*Whenever you think you want to leave your wife or
your girlfriend, think about your child, and how you
want her to grow up. I care about myself, but I would*

*do anything for her. Don't ever be mean to her or neglect her, just love her, and when she gets older, she will give the love back to you.*

*I used to be in the gangs, but it feels better not being with the guys. I don't have many friends around here any more because they're all in the gangs. If you're older, it's not hard to get out of the gang. Me, I just walked away. No gang has ever had control over me. I was pressured into drugs but not to shoot this guy or that guy. All the younger guys are like that now. I don't want to be like that. I decided to stay off the gangs.*

*I feel good about myself now. I used to be real heavy into drugs. I stopped as soon as I started trying to get back with Maurine. I changed right away because I figured who would want someone using drugs and with the gang? There's no use getting back to her if you're going to do all that.*

*We fought too much. We were getting along, but I was getting jealous a lot. I don't know why. Then she decided to move out. It's different now. We're friends, and I'll continue being as close to Genny as I can.*

Miguel

Having a child drastically changes the lives of fathers as well as mothers. Yes, a father can walk away, and some fathers do just that. Other fathers, like Miguel, know that dad, as well as mother, will be ahead if he truly shares the parenting responsibilities along with the joys of rearing his child.

Whether or not you live with your child, the more involved you are in his life, the better your relationship will be.

*He needs less food than he did his first year.*

# Mealtime
# for Toddlers

*Shawna likes to feed herself. She eats regularly, and she eats until she's full. If she puts something in her mouth and she doesn't like the taste, she spits it right out.*

*Between meals she only wants to eat when someone else is eating. I know if I give her too much between meals it will spoil her appetite.*

*She's been on table food most of the time since she was ten months old, and she hasn't had allergic reactions to anything. She usually eats whatever we eat.*

*We eat at home more than we eat out. If we go out to eat, I try to find something good for them. Taking them out is too hard, so we don't do it much.*

Mary, 21 - Shawna, 4; Ahmud, 20 months

Many adults consider eating an enjoyable pastime. Some of us enjoy it too much! But for many small children, mealtime becomes a hassle, a fight with mother and dad.

"Eat your meat right now."

"Just one more bite of green beans."

"No dessert for you until you finish your carrots!"

A toddler's mealtime doesn't have to be a bad experience for everyone. Toddlers have the same kinds of food needs as the rest of us. They need nutritious foods from the Basic Four food groups. They also need a relaxed, friendly atmosphere at mealtime. Both needs are important, as Esteban points out:

*Nathan eats pretty good. He likes vegetables. I used to get all nervous trying to feed him, and it seems to me the kid knows when you're nervous and you just get more nervous. Instead, you want to make it fun while they eat.*

Esteban, 19 - Nathan, 28 months; Ralph, 10 months

## She Can Eat With You

By now, your child can probably eat her meals with you. With a little planning, most of your easy-to-chew food should be suitable for her. Cut meat, fish, and vegetables into finger-sized cubes.

If you're frying food for your family, it's better for your toddler if you broil or dry-fry her food in a non-stick pan. Serve her food before you add the spices or the rich sauce. Foods to avoid completely at this age include popcorn and nuts or any food that might cause her to choke.

*She eats everything in sight. She's a little pig. She's never been finicky. I think it's because everyone else eats everything. We never had a problem with her eating.*

*We don't let her drink a lot of soda, and she's allergic to milk, so we give her the lactaid which is a liquid she drinks with every meal.*

*She often eats two help- ings of dinner. She loves hamburger. Food has never been a battle, and I think that has a lot to do with grandma. Up here we don't have that many fast food places, so we do a lot of home cooking.*

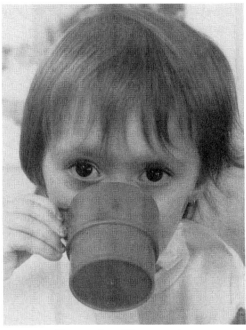
She needs milk every day.

Cathi, 18 - Susie, 34 months

Convenience foods such as canned soups are not as nutritious as foods you prepare yourself. Soups and other dehydrated meals usually contain more salt than your child should have. These foods also contain a variety of preserva- tives, colorings, and artificial flavorings. It's all right to serve them occasionally, but a steady diet of already- prepared foods is not especially good for any of us. Neither is a steady diet of fast foods.

## Offer Small Helpings

Give her small helpings of food. Don't worry if she doesn't seem to eat much. She doesn't need as much as she did six months ago when she was growing so much faster than she is now. She needs daily:

- Twenty ounces of milk
- Fruits and vegetables
- Bread and cereal
- Protein foods

If she doesn't drink enough milk, put it in puddings and soups. Does she like cheese? Let cheese take the place of some of her milk. Cottage cheese and yogurt are also good replacements.

While most toddlers insist on feeding themselves, you may find she occasionally insists just as strongly that you feed her. That's all right. She may not be feeling well, or she may simply be tired of feeding herself all the time.

Allow plenty of time for your toddler to eat. Rushing through a meal is not her style. She'll eat many foods with her fingers, but by her second birthday, she'll be able to handle a spoon quite well.

## Coping with Messiness

Learning to use a spoon is hard work and takes a lot of practice. He has to try. If mother insists on neatness at the table, he'll be discouraged. While he's learning, it's impossible for him to be neat.

*When Derek eats and he's through, he's through. You'd better get him down fast—or he'll throw his food and jump out of his high chair!*

Laurette, 17 - Derek, 18 months

When he eats a cracker, he may first gum it. Then he'll rub the mess all over his face and into his hair. There is no reason to let him sit on the couch while he makes this mess, of course, but his high chair can be cleaned up.

Put a thick layer of newspapers on the floor under his chair to catch the spills. Roll them up after dinner and throw them away. Then you have only your toddler and his chair to clean.

He is fairly easily washed, although he may not appreciate your efforts. If you give him a second washcloth to use on himself while you clean him up, it may help. Try not to let the mess upset you.

Some parents are so horrified at the mess their toddler makes while eating that they don't want anyone else around at mealtime. That's okay. Because of the mess, some people feed toddlers before the rest of the family eats. This is undoubtedly better

*Toddlers do **not** eat neatly!*

than scolding the child throughout dinner for his absolutely normal messiness.

If you realize how normal this messiness is, and that it will happen at this age, you can probably handle it without too much frustration.

By now, your child will probably be drinking most of his milk from a cup or small glass. If you fill it only one-fourth full, the inevitable spilling will be less of a disaster. You can refill it—one-fourth full—as often as he wants it. Be sure you encourage him to drink plenty of milk.

## Toddler Needs Less Food

Remember that your toddler's appetite is much less this year than last. She's not growing nearly as fast as she did those first twelve months.

It is during this stage that many mothers decide their toddlers are "terrible eaters." "She just doesn't eat a thing," they say.

*Meghan is not a good eater. She practically won't touch anything. All she wants is a glass of milk constantly, and it worries me so. I told the doctor about it. She laughed and said, "Oh, I can tell you're going through the fun stage."*

*"What can I do about it?" I asked. She said to give Meghan vitamins with iron, and that seemed to help her appetite. She also told me to quit fussing about it.*

*I try to avoid candy because I don't like to give them too many sweets. Sometimes when Meghan doesn't want to eat, I think it's because she's too busy to bother. She does love pizza.*

Louise, 19 - Meghan, 23 months; Mark, 5½ months

Don't try to force or even coax her to eat. Offer small servings of nutritious food. Don't offer sweets at all. If she seems to need an in-between-meal snack, make it part of her daily food plan.

Carrots, orange juice, graham crackers, milk, and apple are examples of good snack foods that won't pave the way for your lovely child to become a fat adult. If you overfeed now, remember, she is likely to have a weight problem when she's grown. You don't want your child to spend her life fighting unhealthy, unattractive fat.

*Sean snacks a lot—plums, grapes, nectarines, peaches. He doesn't eat much candy and other sweets. I won't let him. He doesn't need any candy*

*because of his teeth, and because it would spoil his
appetite.*

Ginger, 18 - Sean, 17 months

If she doesn't want to eat any lunch at all, calmly take
her food away. She won't starve by suppertime. Just don't
tide her over with a handful of cookies an hour later.

If she eats all her food and asks for more, give it to her
in the same way, without an emotional reaction. Whether
she eats all her food or not is not what makes her a
"good girl."

## Serving New Foods

*There are a lot of things he won't eat. He doesn't
like vegetables. I put them on his plate every night,
but if he doesn't eat, I don't force it. My mother is
more like, "You have to make him eat," but I don't.*

Jessica, 17 - Craig, 30 months

Your toddler may appear to like only a few foods. When
you offer him a new food, he may refuse even to taste it.
Rather than insisting he "clean his plate," serve yourself the
same food and show him you like to eat it. Suggest that he
might taste it. If he refuses, however, it's okay. There's no
need to bribe, force, or push.

Research shows that children who are bribed to eat new
foods are less likely to eat that food later than are those
who simply are served the food with no bribe involved.

Serve the new food again a few days later. He may be
willing to try it, but don't make a fuss if he doesn't. Absolutely nothing is accomplished when mom or dad demands
that the child eat the food.

Your child is in control at this point. *You, however, are
in control of the foods served.* You don't need to serve soda
or other junk foods in your home.

Continue offering her the variety of foods the rest of your family is eating. You may say she won't eat any vegetables at all. What about raw ones? She can get even more vitamins from raw vegetables than from cooked ones.

Until she's two, however, don't give her raw carrot sticks or other hard-to-chew foods because she might choke. If she likes raw carrots, grate them for her.

Hot dogs may be an all-American food, but they really shouldn't be given to toddlers because of the risk of choking. Even if you slit the skin or slice them into little circles, your child could choke on a piece of hotdog. Besides, hot dogs are high in fat.

Meals and snacks need to be at about the same time every day. Toddlers have small stomachs, and they get hungry within a couple of hours after a meal. If he refuses to eat at mealtime, then asks for a snack immediately afterward, it's generally best not to give it to him. Tell him he must wait until snack time.

*It's important that she enjoy mealtime.*

# Outlaw Junk Food

*She has always eaten good. I let her munch if she wants to—whole wheat and peanut butter crackers, but no junk at all. I used to have problems with my teeth, and I don't want her to. I think junk food is so bad for you. I used to always eat stuff like that. No cokes. My doctor said if you pour coke on a car, it will eat the paint right off!*

Ione, 18 - Lori, 14 months

Keep the junk food away from your picky eater. If he isn't hungry enough for meals, he certainly doesn't need a soda, potato chips, or even cookies an hour later. While one or two oatmeal cookies provide a little nutrition, a handful of sugary snacks won't do much for him except ruin his appetite for more nutritious foods.

If you're in your own home, or if the people you live with are willing, don't keep junk food there at all. If you don't have candy and cookies in the cupboard or soft drinks in the refrigerator, your toddler can't have them while he's at home. The occasional sweet he gets from the outside world won't matter that much as long as you aren't providing them, too.

# Fat-Proofing Your Toddler

If you have a toddler who already appears overweight, don't put him on a reducing diet. Do, however, guide his eating so that he gains weight more slowly. Make a list of the food he eats in a three-day period. You may be surprised at the amount of high-calorie food he consumes.

Don't cut out the meat, vegetables, milk, fruit, and cereal, his Basic Four foods. Get serious about not having junk food in the house. If he drinks more than a quart of milk a day, try diluting it with water. Most doctors don't recommend skim or low-fat milk for children under two.

Encourage your overweight toddler to get more exercise. Do you take walks, but push him in his stroller? Get him to walk with you. Is he outdoors enough? It may take extra energy on your part to get him to a park if you don't have a yard, but it may well be worth the effort.

Both Dawn and her daughter, Mercedes, 3, are quite overweight. Dawn's food habits probably explain both her own and her daughter's weight problem. Like all children, Mercedes mimics her mother. She, too, eats a lot of junk food, then is "picky," as her mother says, at mealtime.

*I'm a big junk food eater, a nervous eater, and I pick all the time. A lot of foods you're supposed to have I don't even like.*

*I like my bacon, fried potatoes, toast and butter, the eggs—but they have to be done in grease. For lunch I seldom just make sandwiches for us. It's McDonald's. If we don't eat breakfast we usually go to McDonald's and then have something here. We do hit the ice cream man.*

*Mercedes doesn't eat enough to do anything. In the morning she'll have a bowl of cereal or a couple of pieces of bacon. She doesn't like eggs and doesn't care much for potatoes. At lunch if we go to McDonald's she'll eat half of a half of a hamburger, plus a half bag of fries, maybe half of her drink. With dinner she will eat at the most 10 tiny squares of meat.*

Dawn, 19 - Mercedes, 3

Mark and Kelly Ellen were eating a lot of junk food. When they realized that Dustin was copying their poor food habits, they decided to change their ways. Mark explained:

*For three or four months Dustin had cola all the time. He'd go through all the sodas. The same with*

*Twinkies and cakes. We were drinking a lot of cola
and had potato chips everywhere.*

*Then we realized all that junk food was getting
expensive and we were both gaining weight, so we
started a little diet. Now we don't even buy sodas.
Now we're real conscious about what we eat, and the
same goes for him. For the last year or so, we won't
give him junk food. We learned from experience. If he
has candy all day, he gets higher and crankier.*

*Junk food is like a lot of other things. If it's there
and it's annoying, just take it away. As you take it
away, explain why he can't have it. If we had a box
full of cakes and cookies, he'd be into it. So we
stopped having junk in the house.*

Mark, 20 - Dustin, 30 months (Kelly Ellen, 20)

## It's Your Responsibility

You have three basic responsibilities connected with
feeding your child:

• You need to offer him the nutritious food he needs.

• Help him learn that mealtime is a pleasant, sociable
time. It's not a period of coaxing him to eat, or a
time to argue with the rest of the family.

• Help him stay at a healthy weight.

Your modeling is all important in the development of
your toddler's food habits. If you're a picky eater, or if you
survive mostly on junk food, you can expect your child to
do the same thing. If you're careful to eat foods from the
Basic Four food groups at each meal, your child is more
likely to eat well too.

When this happens, payoff is high in terms of your
toddler's health and general development. Her disposition
is likely to be better, too, because she'll feel better if she
eats the foods she needs.

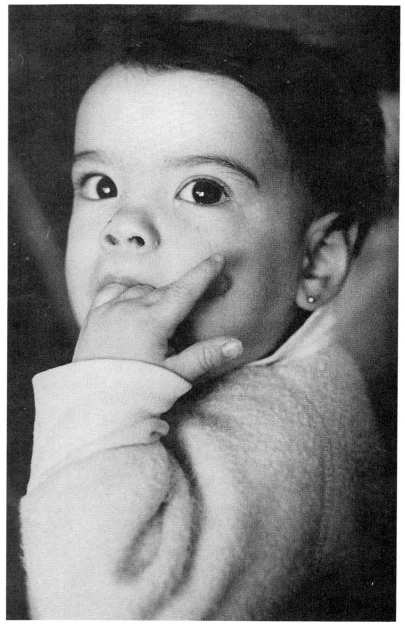

*A bedtime ritual with mom or dad helps avoid bedtime problems.*

# Importance of Sleep

*She usually goes to bed at 7:30 or 8:00. It's not like whenever she goes to bed, it's okay. It's better for her to have a schedule.*

*She doesn't fight me. She knows when she has to go to bed. I help her with her PJs, brush her teeth, then usually lie down and talk with her or read a book, or tell her what we'll do the next morning.*

Shalimar, 19 - Ellie, 30 months

## Sleep/Rest Important for Toddlers

Your toddler will be less cranky if she eats and sleeps, or at least rests, at regular times. You also need time for yourself. Her daytime naps help both of you.

Most toddlers continue taking a fairly long afternoon nap. Some, however, may not want to nap. It's best to put her to bed anyway, together with her favorite stuffed toy and some books. If she doesn't go to sleep, an hour of quiet play will refresh her for the rest of the day.

## Sleep Time

Generally, toddlers don't have a particularly difficult time getting to sleep at night. Now that they get around easily, they fill their day with activity. By evening they're usually tired and ready for sleep. However, this isn't always the case.

Sleep problems can occur at any age. Sometimes at around a year, a baby who was fairly easy to get down for sleep may suddenly start having a difficult time. He may resist everything about getting ready for bed. At this age, he enjoys being with his parents, and he doesn't want to leave them. He doesn't want to be alone.

When toddlers hit the "I'll do it myself" stage, complete with lots of "No," bedtime may once again become a problem.

*Bedtime is a hassle. Henry won't go to bed before I do, and he won't go in his crib. For the last couple of months, he has been in bed with me. If I put him in his crib, he cries and climbs out of it. He goes to sleep with me, then I put him in his crib.*

*He has his bath after he eats dinner. I put his pajamas on him and get him ready for bed. Then he wants to go outside, and he gets all dirty again.*

*He goes to bed when we do, but at 6:30 in the morning he doesn't want to get up. Today I brought him to school asleep. I couldn't wake him up.*

*He used to go to bed earlier. I think the change was when he quit taking a bottle and started playing outside more.*

Olivia, 20 - Henry, 23 months

Henry is like most toddlers. He's so busy playing and learning about his world that he doesn't want to take time to sleep. His parents should decide on the time they feel he should be in bed, then see that he gets there at that time.

Getting Henry ready for bed, then allowing him to go outside to play doesn't help him settle down to sleep. If they bathe him a little later and develop a more elaborate bedtime routine with him, he may fall asleep more easily.

## Importance of Bedtime Ritual

Parents often start a bedtime routine when their child is six or eight months old. They find it helps their child settle down to sleep without a lot of fussing. If this isn't working as well now, the solution may be an even more complicated bedtime ritual.

*Whatever her routine,*
*woe to you if you upset it!*

Quiet play, a little snack, a relaxing bath, and looking at a book, with perhaps a lullaby or two, might be a part of your child's ritual for falling asleep. Turning on a night light or some soft music may help too. One little girl had a certain corner of her blanket which she rubbed on her cheek while she sucked her thumb. To her parent's amazement, she could find that one corner even in the dark.

Six months ago, perhaps you read to her, rocked her a few minutes, and put her to bed with her teddy bear. Now she has to have a drink before she kisses you, not after. She may want the same story every night. Perhaps she has to tell each toy "Night-night." Whatever her routine, woe to you if you upset it!

*Derek sometimes drives me up the wall when he*
*won't go to sleep. He has this one blanket that he has*

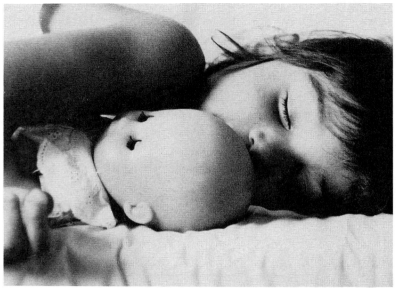

*Her favorite doll helps her settle down to sleep.*

*to have to go to bed. He's had it all his life. Every-
body calls him Linus.*

*I'll say, "Where's your blanket?" and he'll go get
it. He'll get a diaper for me, and I'll clap. Then he'll
lie down so I can change him.*

                                    Laurette, 17 - Derek, 18 months

This ritual, if she feels she's in charge, can be a good
compromise. You get what you want when she goes to bed
without a huge fuss. You each give up something, too. You
take the time to go through the ritual with her, and she goes
to bed. So don't try to get out of that bedtime story once in
awhile just because you're tired. It's important to her.

## Solving Bedtime Problems
If your child already has a problem going to bed, the
solution may not be easy. One young mother, whose

husband recently joined the Navy, moved in with her
parents-in-law for two months. She then decided she and
her daughter would be better off in their own home. But
Esperanza's child didn't adapt to coming back home as
well as she had hoped:

> *Juanita is a crybaby now. She is really spoiled
> because I've been at Ruben's mother's house. She got
> a lot of attention there.*
>
> *When I came back home, I couldn't give her that
> much attention because I have to do a lot of things
> here. She won't stay in her crib to take a nap. She just
> screams. I either take her out and set her here in the
> living room, or I leave her in there and she screams.*
>
> *She used to sleep three or four hours each after-
> noon. Over there she would sleep only 45 minutes or
> so. Before, she was always happy, but now she isn't.
> She has changed, and I don't understand why.*
>
> *When Juanita was four months old, I got real
> attached to her because Ruben was gone. I always
> had her by me, and I spent my whole time with her.*
>
> *She hates that crib now, but I hate to put her on my
> bed. She sleeps with me a lot. When Ruben comes
> home, I guess I'll have to let her sleep with us.*
>
> *I should start getting her used to the crib and let
> her cry. She takes a bottle when she goes to bed. She
> drinks her bottle, then wriggles around for thirty
> minutes before she settles down to sleep.*
>
> Esperanza, 17 - Juanita, 12 months

Juanita has had more change than she likes in her first
year of living. First, daddy was home. Then he left. Then
Juanita and mother moved in with a family consisting of
grandma, grandpa, and several young aunts and uncles.

Now she's back in the apartment with her mother and her other grandma who is gone most of the time.

She's not sure what's going on in her world. First, she needs a terrific amount of love from mother. But mother is lonely and unhappy because daddy is gone. It's a difficult situation any way you look at it.

If Esperanza really wants Juanita to sleep in her crib, perhaps she should insist—and insist over and over again—that she sleep there.

At the same time, she needs to try extra hard to help Juanita feel secure again.

## She Doesn't Want to Be Alone

If a baby cries when she's put to bed, it's probably because she doesn't want to be there. She doesn't want to be there because she doesn't want to be alone. She would far rather stay out in the living room with her parents. She may feel a bit deserted when she's in bed by herself and mom or dad has shut the door firmly behind her.

One "solution" often tried when baby cries is to get her up again, hoping that in time she will quiet down enough to go to sleep. With this method, she gets to be up with you. She learns that if she cries, she can get up. Why should she go to bed tomorrow night without fussing?

The opposite "solution" is to shut the door even more firmly and leave her alone to cry. A few minutes of crying won't hurt her. If she's tired enough, she'll go to sleep, exactly what you want.

Some toddlers, however, will cry and cry for a couple of hours if left alone. They may fall asleep from exhaustion, but they're not likely to sleep well after such an ordeal. This is the kind of crying Esperanza described. Her solution was to let Juanita sleep with her on her bed. But that wasn't the solution Esperanza wanted.

## Every-Five-Minute Routine

A sensible approach could be a combination of the first two methods. When she cries, go in to see her. Tell her "Good night," pat her back a minute, then walk out. If she continues crying, repeat the process five minutes later. Continue going back in to reassure her every five minutes until she goes to sleep.

*A tired toddler is often a miserable toddler.*

She may cry for another hour, but she knows you haven't left her because she's seen you every five minutes. She also knows she won't be brought back into the living room after bedtime.

This method, according to Penelope Leach, author of *Your Baby and Child from Birth to Age Five* (1989: Alfred A. Knopf), will almost always work. Within a week at the most, your toddler should be much more accepting of her bedtime.

Why make such a fuss? Why not let her stay up until she decides she's ready to go to bed? As mentioned before, most toddlers become utterly exhausted before they will give in to sleep. A tired toddler is often a miserable toddler.

A young mother in our school's parenting class described the problem she was having in getting her 14-month-old son to go to bed and to sleep at night. He would get up again and again. He wouldn't go to sleep until very late. In desperation, she often allowed him to stay up far longer than she wanted—for his sake and for her own.

I suggested she try the go-in-every-five-minutes-and-pat-his-back routine as a possible solution.

Two days later Jamie returned to report that the every-five-minutes routine had worked. She added, "I was so exhausted after those first two nights I couldn't get up to

come to school!" The third night, she said, Austin was
asleep twenty minutes after she put him to bed.

## Night Waking

*If he wakes, instead of handing him a bottle,
offer him a cup of water.
Tell him "Good night" and walk away.*

Occasionally young mothers spoke of giving their year-
old children several bottles during the night. If he has a
bottle at bedtime, he doesn't need the extra food. Again,
remember the danger of tooth decay if your child sleeps
with a bottle of milk.

If he wakes, instead of handing him a bottle, offer him a
cup of water. Tell him "Good night" and walk away. If he
continues crying, try the every-five-minute routine for a
week. You'll be exhausted, but if he starts sleeping through
the night, think how much better you'll feel the next week.

Your toddler may have a nightmare occasionally. After
he's asleep, you hear him screaming. When you go in, he
may be kicking or moving frantically. He needs you to
reassure him that you're there, that it was only a bad dream.

Go in and talk to him for a minute. Perhaps he would
like a drink of water. When he calms down and isn't afraid
anymore, tell him "Good night" and go back to bed.

## Should Child Sleep with Parent?

"Should" you sleep with your child? Most child development experts in our culture say "No." Some people, however, believe otherwise. Some parents feel it's easier to
sleep with their toddler. Perhaps they just like having the
child sleep in bed with them. As long as everyone is able to
sleep well, it doesn't seem to matter.

*Toddlers may sleep better if the day includes active outdoor play.*

However, there may be some problems. One parent or the other may not be able to get enough rest. Then, of course, there is the issue of privacy. Children should not observe lovemaking. Also, once this pattern has become established, it may be very difficult to stop.

Having their child sleep with them was described as a "problem" by several of the young parents interviewed.

> *One thing I did that I wish I hadn't was letting Heidi sleep with me. When she was little, a newborn, I took her to bed with me. She didn't like her crib very much. She would sleep with me all night, and my mom would say, "You have to put her in that crib or she won't ever sleep in it."*
>
> *She was right. At about five months, I put her in her crib and let her sleep by herself. She didn't like that at all, but after a couple of weeks she was okay. Dennis feels pretty strong about not wanting Heidi to sleep with us.*

*I have a suggestion for mothers of newborns. If*
*they breastfeed and have the child in bed with them,*
*they should, after they feed him, put him in his*
*own bed.*

Jenny, 18 - Heidi, 13 months

Sometimes a mother feels she has no choice but to sleep
with her baby. There's no room otherwise.

*Gary wakes up about three times each night. I give*
*him a bottle and change him. He sleeps with me.*

*I had no choice. I didn't want him to, but we moved*
*here when he was about 1 1/2 months old, and there*
*was no place for the crib. I had to store it away, so he*
*slept with me. Then a month ago my sister moved out,*
*and there was room for the crib. I put it up the other*
*day, but he won't sleep in it.*

*He is really attached to me at night. He won't go to*
*sleep until I do. I hope he outgrows it.*

Jan, 15, - Gary, 12 months

Although Gary has already formed a strong habit of
sleeping with his mother, Jan has three choices.

She can continue letting him sleep with her. Perhaps he
will eventually outgrow it, as she hopes. The danger here is
that his mother may suddenly decide at a later time that she
doesn't want him in bed with her. It may be even harder to
get him to sleep elsewhere then.

She can let him go to sleep in her bed, then move him to
his crib. If she chooses this method, she should tell him
what she will be doing. She might say, "You may go to
sleep in my bed. After you're asleep, I'll move you into
your own bed where you will sleep the rest of the night."

Another solution is to insist he sleep in his crib now. Jan
could follow the check-on-him-every-five-minutes routine
described previously. It will be difficult both for her and for
Gary, but it might be worth the effort.

Brigette found a fairly simple solution to a similar problem:

>  *Rudy has slept with me at least three-fourths of his life. It got to the point where he wouldn't go to sleep until I was in bed with him. I would lie down with him for about an hour until he was asleep. I strongly recommend you not sleep with your kids—except when they're sick, of course.*
>
>  *Now I'll be marrying John, and I don't want Rudy to think John is kicking him out of my bed. A friend suggested I get him a new bed and make a big deal of it. She said I should do this long before my wedding. Then when I get married, it will all be done.*
>
>  *I bought Rudy a youth bed. He was thrilled, and it worked. He goes to sleep by himself in his own bed now.*
>
>  Brigette, 22 - Joy, 4; Rudy, 3

## Remember—Routine Helps

Helping her learn to eat and sleep at regular hours is almost certain to improve your child's disposition. In fact, the "spoiled" toddler who whines a lot and is generally demanding may improve a great deal if she is put on a reasonable time schedule.

With careful planning and your willingness to develop a bedtime routine for your child and to stick to that routine every night, bedtime can be a pleasant experience for you and your child. It can be a time of special closeness between you, a time you both may cherish.

*He loves having grandma read to him.*

# CHAPTER 8

# Living with Extended Family

*My mother has been a great help in all this from the beginning. She takes Sharon to school. She also picks her up and takes care of her until I get home.*

*I don't spend as much time with Sharon as I'd like, but I like my job, and it pays good. I'm trying very hard to become somebody important—not fame-wise or anything like that. I just want to make it and survive all of life's problems. I'm doing fine now.*

Marlys 19 - Sharon, 3

Often, being with family is the best possible situation for young parents. If you're with your parents because you aren't old enough and/or can't afford a place of your own, however, you may feel trapped. You'd rather not be there, but you have no choice. The feeling of being trapped is hard to live with, but the support which a family can give often makes it possible to weather the ups and downs of being a teen parent.

Many young parents interviewed for this book saw good points in three-generation living. They also described problems brought about by lack of independence for themselves. They found it difficult to play the role of somebody's child when, at the same time, they were working hard at being somebody else's parent.

> *I had the support of my parents when I needed them. When I was sick, they were there. They helped out on expenses. It was good because it helped us get a start financially. But it was also as if the three of us didn't have our own life. "Where are you going? What time will you get home?"*
>
> *You can take only so much of being married and, at the same time, being treated like a child again. We lived with them for a year.*
>
> Rosemarie, 19 - Helen, 3

## Parents' Support Is Crucial

Jill is parenting Todd alone. His father left when he learned of Jill's pregnancy. Jill is now in college, and she believes her parents' support is extremely important:

> *My parents have been good about everything. They don't put much pressure on me. My mom is such a big help. If they weren't like this, I probably wouldn't even be in college now. They want me to get my education, too.*
>
> *Sometimes it gets frustrating, but somehow it kind of evens out. My dad will say you shouldn't do this or that. I'm not one to keep my mouth shut, but we haven't gotten into any big arguments yet. Mostly my dad is kidding so it doesn't bother me too much.*

*I imagine sometimes it will be hard. I've read where single parents living with their parents get very upset and just leave. I really respect my mom and dad for what they've done for me.*

Jill, 18 - Todd, 16 months

Darla talked about the advantages of living with her parents and about her concern that Janis is being spoiled:

*Of course there are advantages in living with your family. Janis is learning to talk quicker because everybody is talking to her. She's really athletic and into sports already. She counts, knows most of her alphabet, her colors. She learns a lot because everybody teaches her.*

*But she's spoiled. My mom—if I scold Janis, grandma will baby her. She'll run to grandma.*

Darla, 17 - Janis, 2

In many three-generation families, disagreement over discipline is a major problem. The child becomes confused and often appears undisciplined because he doesn't know whether to listen to mom or grandma. Often he appears to listen to neither.

The importance of the child's parents and their parents agreeing on discipline is discussed in more detail in *Teens Parenting—Discipline from Birth to Three.*

## There May Be Difficulties

When several people live together, disagreements will come up. Those disagreements may occur frequently if the household consists of a teenager, her/his child, and the grandparents. Often, the grandparents feel they should be in charge because, after all, they have already reared a family. At the same time, the child's parents will undoubtedly feel they should be in control. Conflict often occurs:

*What I can't stand is when we walk in and we already have eaten, and they tell me to set Derek down and feed him. I say he has eaten, and she says, "What?"*

*I say "Pizza," and she says that's not good for him.*

---

## This is their house, I'm still under age, and we all have to adjust.

---

*Or she tells me it's too hot to have him in the water. They make me feel like I'm doing everything wrong. I don't know everything, but they don't know everything either. If I say "Black," they say "White."*

*This is their house, I'm still under age, and we all have to adjust. I get real up-tight when they're on my case. I have to be careful not to take it out on Derek.*

                                        Laurette, 17 - Derek, 18 months

Sometimes the fact that the house is more crowded because of the baby creates extra problems. Grandma may want the same rules followed that she remembers using when her children were little. If the baby must share a room with other family members, things get complicated:

*My mom doesn't bug me, but she's making me feel like I don't know what I'm doing, like I'm a little kid. For example, Shelly never got used to the crib.*

*She's in my room with my cousin, and they keep coming in and out, turning on the light, and waking her. So I pick her up and take her in where I sleep, but my mom says I'll have problems later on. I tell her I can't help it, that I have to get some sleep so I can go to school. She'll sleep there for about two hours, but not the whole night.*

*If Shelly had the room by herself, I would let her
alone.*

Dixie, 18 - Shelly, 17 months

Dixie appears to have worked out a rather good solution.
Perhaps she needs to share with her mom her reasons for
moving Shelly into her room. She might even consider
moving Shelly's crib into her room.

It's nice if parent and child can have separate rooms, but
often this isn't possible. Shelly might be able to go to sleep
more easily if she is routinely put in her crib in Dixie's
room. Expecting a toddler to sleep while other children go
in and out of the room is expecting a lot.

## Compromise Is Needed

Even young parents who realize the benefits of living
with their parents for awhile often have mixed feelings
about the situation. During the toddler stage, when baby is
into everything, feelings may get especially tense. Glorianne's parents didn't think it was necessary to child-proof
their house, for example.

Danny was an extra lively toddler, however, and
Glorianne disagreed:

*Child-proofing is important at the one-year-old
stage. You have to teach them not to touch some
things, but there is no point in having endless
temptations for them to get into trouble.*

*It took awhile to get my parents to agree, but
finally I got some of the things put away. We made
sure Danny was never in the living room so nothing
in there was ever touched. In the den my mom put
some things up. A lot of times when we were in there
together playing I would put more things out of his
reach until we were done. Then I'd put them back.*

*He could explore within his limits, and that didn't
frustrate anybody else. And he did learn not to touch.*

                                        Glorianne, 19 - Danny, 4

Glorianne illustrates the value of compromise. Because
she was willing to keep Danny out of the living room, her
parents were willing to have part of their home child-
proofed for awhile.

## The Problem of Candy

A surprising number of young parents talked about their
concern because grandma thinks the baby should have
candy and other foods his mother doesn't believe are good
for him.

*Janis doesn't like to eat a whole lot, or even at all
sometimes. So my mom will resort to sweet cereal so
she'll eat. I know if you wait until she's hungry, she'll
eat what we have. They give her ice cream and candy,
and she's going to get cavities too soon. My mom
says, "She needs something in her stomach," but all it
is is sugar.*

                                                    Darla

*Shelly doesn't snack a lot except when she sees
somebody eating something. She has very little candy.
First of all, she makes a mess, and besides, I don't
want her to get cavities. I don't give her soft drinks
either, just orange juice or apple juice.*

*Everybody tells me, "You're so mean, you don't
give her any candy. When she gets older, she's going
to see all that candy and eat it all."*

*Even my mother tells me I'm so mean. She makes
herself sound like she knows more than I do. She used
to always give candy to Shelly behind my back. One
time they were eating chocolates, and I told Shelly*

*she couldn't have any. Then she walked by me, and
she had chocolate all over her mouth.*

*It makes me feel bad. I feel like telling them to
mind their own business, but I can't do that. Mom's
beginning to do more of that, and it's getting to me.
It's building up, and I know I'll wind up telling her
something I shouldn't.*

Dixie

If this is happening in your home, perhaps you could try
talking with your family. Could you work out a change?
If your family doesn't know much about nutrition, perhaps
you could tactfully provide some help on the subject of
feeding toddlers. There are lots of well-written and brief
pamphlets as well as whole books on this topic.

Do you eat a lot of junk food? If you set a good example
for your child by eating mostly nutritious foods, your
family may be more likely to respect your wishes
concerning your child's nutrition.

If you aren't already doing much of the food preparation,
could you offer to help more with the understanding that
your child is not to be given junk food?

Of course you know your family, and you can probably
come up with better ideas for changing the situation.

## Problems When You Leave

If you move in with your child's other parent and his/her
family, you may find it difficult to adjust. Kris barely knew
Mick's parents when she started living with them.

Mick lived about 50 miles away from Kris, so they
didn't see each other often. Actually, through a misunder-
standing, they split when Cassandra was ten months old.
Soon, however, they started talking by phone. The day after
Kris graduated from high school, Mick was at her door.
Was she ready to leave?

*Grandma and grandpa will miss them when they leave.*

*We sat outside and talked for three hours. We decided Cassie and I should be living with him, so we got my stuff, and we left. My mother was angry. She yelled and told me I always had things my way, that I never thought about her. All that time she had helped me, she said, and I didn't appreciate her.*

*As we left, my dad yelled at Mick, "Don't you ever come back."*

*That first month was awful. When I moved in with Mick's folks, Mick and I hadn't seen each other at all for three or four months. We hardly knew each other, and I didn't know his family before that.*

*It was especially hard because Mick and I were brought up differently. We're both Mexican, but his parents are from Mexico and mine are from Texas. His parents speak only Spanish while mine speak English plus Spanish. My parents always had enough money to get me everything I needed while his parents have lots of kids, and it's hard to stretch the money.*

> *It's hard, and that's one thing we argue about. My
> mom is always buying Cassie things and giving me
> money while his parents can't do that.*
>
> *Even though I had seen his parents only a few
> times before I moved in, they seemed to take a liking
> to me right away. Mick's brothers and sisters are all
> younger, and I started walking them to school every
> morning. They liked that, and Cassie and I enjoyed it.*
>
> *We're still with Mick's parents, and it's working
> well. They kind of stand back and let it flow.*
>
> Kris, 17 - Cassandra, 25 months

Kris was wise to step in immediately and walk Mick's
little brothers and sisters to school. By doing so, she
showed her willingness to be an active part of the family. It also gave her a chance to get acquainted quickly
with Mick's siblings as she took over one of his
mother's daily tasks.

The move apparently worked out well for Kris and
Cassandra although Cassie still misses her other
grandparents:

> *Leaving my folks' home was hard on Cassandra
> too, and it still is. When we get in the car, she's
> always saying, "Let's go see grandma." She loves her
> so much.*
>
> Kris

Even if your parents were absolutely horrified at your
pregnancy, they probably dearly love your child. If you
have lived with them during your baby's early months or
years, leaving is likely to be hard on both baby and
grandparents.

Even if you have taken most of the responsibility for
caring for your child, he surely has bonded strongly with
your parents, too. They will miss him when he leaves.

# Winning Over the Other Parents

Whether or not you live with your partner's parents, you
probably want your child to be able to enjoy his grandparents. Sometimes those grandparents need to be won
over. Kristin faced this situation:

> *When she learned I was pregnant, Stan's mother
> told him not to see me again, to give the baby up and
> go into the Marines as he had planned. "Don't let her
> interfere," she told him.*
>
> *The first time I saw Stan's mom was at the hospital
> because she didn't want her neighbors to know I was
> pregnant. She didn't want her family to know, and she
> didn't want her church to know. She wanted me to
> stay out of sight.*
>
> *Stan and I decided to get married a couple of
> months after Ryan was born. His mother tried to plan
> our wedding. I think the closest we ever came to
> splitting was when I put my foot down and said, "If
> you want to plan this wedding with your mother, then
> marry your mother. If you want to marry me, we'll
> plan it together."*
>
> Kristin, 24 - Ryan, 8; Tiana, 4

Kristin, however, decided she wouldn't accept a poor
relationship with her husband's parents. They needed to get
along for Ryan's sake, so she took the lead in improving
family relationships:

> *Things started changing after I began taking Ryan
> over there. I got along good with Stan's brothers and
> sisters, so I'd pick a time when they'd be home. I
> would act like it was a normal visit to grandma and
> grandpa. Then Stan started going along with me.*
>
> *I didn't want to explain to Ryan why grandma
> didn't come to visit. I didn't want him to think*

*grandma didn't come over because she didn't love him. I didn't want him to think grandma didn't like me because I got pregnant with him. So I acted normal, and in the long run, it worked. She respects me.*

*Nobody wins if you stay away. I don't know how I knew that would be best, but I knew it would be wrong to drive a bigger wedge, and I didn't want to come between Stan and his mom.*

Kristin

Encouraging positive contact between your child and both sets of grandparents usually is best for the child and for the grandparents. Kristin won over her husband's parents because she was willing to make an effort.

At the time, it would have been easier to say, "They don't like me and I don't like them. That's all there is to it." Instead, she was determined that Ryan would win. In the process, everyone in this family became winners.

Whether you're still living with your parents or you're in your own home, fostering a good relationship between your child and his grandparents is important.

## It Can Work

For Elysha, continuing to live with her parents works:

*I think I'll stay here quite a while. I have my live-in nanny here (my mother). Antoine likes that. I always liked being with my grandmother. Everywhere she went, I went. I'd go to her house for the weekend.*

Elysha, 21 - Antoine, 4

Other young parents prefer to live by themselves, and they work hard to be able to afford to do so. With lots of love, respect and caring among those involved, either way can work for you and your child.

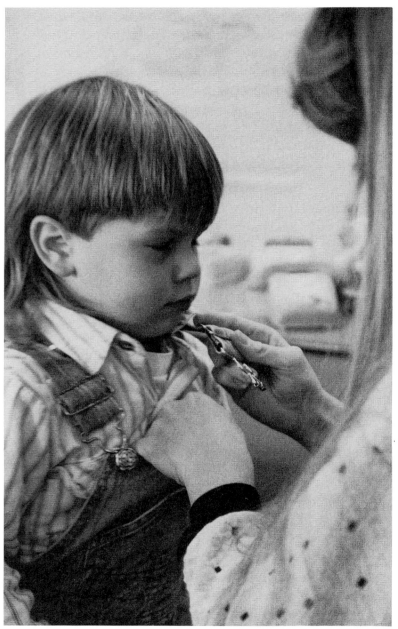

*She's growing up—but she still needs your help occasionally.*

# Your Amazing Two-Year-Old

*Johnnie's not a little baby anymore—he's his own little self. He has his own personality. He doesn't like me to do things for him now, and he's more demanding. If he wants it, he wants it now.*

*I was waiting for him to talk, and now he won't stop. He wants to know about a lot of things.*

*You know how when they're little, they want you to carry them. Now he doesn't want me to grab him. Now he wants to walk. Sometimes I feel sad because he doesn't want me to do a lot of things.*

*He mimics me a lot. When I do my homework, he wants his pencil and his book, and he sits down with me. I'm also watching my language now. If I use a bad word, he's sure to repeat it.*

Natalie, 17 - Johnnie, 26 months

A whole new world opens up to your toddler between her second and third birthdays. She not only has learned to walk and run, but is mastering other skills. She can jump, and she can ride a variety of wheel toys. She is beginning to dress and undress herself. She feeds herself with a little help, and she plays with toys in a much more complex manner. She is fond of crayons and painting.

She loves to imitate the activities of both adults and other children. She will imitate both the way you do want her to behave, and the way you don't want her to behave.

She can talk, and is learning new words rapidly. She can understand most of what is said to her if it is spoken in simple terms, although she won't always interpret it correctly. Her experience with language is limited. What looks like defiance is often simply not understanding what you expect of her.

## Your Child's First Teacher

Do you plan to be a teacher? Whether your answer is yes or no, you're one already. You are your child's first and certainly most important teacher. If he has been in an infant center or is attending preschool, you have help with your teaching job. You still probably have your child with you during a greater part of his day than do his other teachers.

*She's real bright. She's always wanting to learn and know things. She's always asking "Why?" I try to explain to her so she can understand.*

*She watches everything I do now, and she copies me. I brush my hair, and she wants to brush hers. She wants to brush her teeth when I do mine.*

Shalimar, 19 - Ellie, 30 months

As he explores, talk with him. Comment on the things around him. When you go for a walk with him, give him a bag to collect treasures—a little rock, a feather, a dandelion. When you return home, talk with him about these items.

Now you can begin to talk about what happened yesterday and your plans for tomorrow because he is beginning to understand the idea of time.

Read to him again and again and again.

*At night they pick out the books they want to read and I read to them. Shawna kind of knows what the story is because she almost always picks out the same books every night. Her favorites are the Dr. Seuss books. Before I turn the light off she wants to look at the book herself.*

*Ever since she was little, before she could even talk, I've taken her to the library when they have the reading programs. I started when she was six months old.*

*Ahmud gets jealous when he sees me reading, so now he sits down and listens too. Sometimes he gets bored and goes off and looks at his own book. Then he'll come back and want me to read.*

Mary, 21 - Shawna, 4; Ahmud, 20 months

Mary explained why she reads to Shawna every night whether or not she feels like it:

*Sometimes when I'm tired I would just as soon not read, but I don't want them to think if you're tired you don't read. So we read anyway. When they're in school they can't quit reading just because they're tired.*

Mary

Developing language skills is perhaps your child's most important task this year. You help her each time you talk with her, sing to her, tell her stories, and read to her. You

also help her when you listen to her. Encourage her to tell
you stories. Ask her to tell you about the book you've been
reading to her every night for the past month. You may find
she has it memorized! Of course you don't expect her to
actually read for several years yet.

Watching and listening to your child as she develops
speaking ability is exciting. Remember the baby who
could only communicate with you by crying? She's come
a long way!

## "I Love You, Mommy"

You probably are thrilled when your toddler says "I love
you." All parents like those words. Toddlers, however, are
emotional little people whose feelings change quickly. The
"I love you, Mommy" may turn into "I hate you" ten
minutes later because you couldn't allow him to do something he wanted to do. You probably will feel hurt or angry
the first time this happens.

*She loves to play with mommy.*

*Mickey says "No" and tells me I'm not his friend
any more. I tell him I'm his friend and I still love him.
He will say "No, you're not my friend," and walk
away. A few minutes later he comes back and decides
we're friends.*

Susan, 20 - Mickey, 30 months; Felicia, 11 months

Instead of showing your anger, reassure him that you
love him a lot and you're sorry he's feeling that way right
now. Of course you won't let him kick or hurt you when
he's angry—or any other time. Give him a chance to talk
about his feelings if he wants to. Your patience and calm
reaction will help him deal with his anger.

## To Bed, To Sleep?

Fatigue is another factor that influences behavior. Toddlers are very active and tire quickly. Many resist napping.
Simple fatigue is at the root of many behavior problems.
Recognizing this and adjusting expectations may make life
easier for everyone.

If your child doesn't go right to sleep when she goes to
bed, it doesn't necessarily mean she doesn't need to rest.
Most two-year-olds will be better off if they continue their
afternoon naps. If she doesn't want to go to sleep, tell her
that it's all right. She can play quietly in her bed. Give her
some books and a quiet toy. Ask her to play there for an
hour. Chances are she'll go to sleep. If she doesn't, she will
still get the rest she needs.

You'll also appreciate the quiet time. Perhaps you can
nap at the same time. If you're feeling impatient with your
child, a nap for each of you may be the best approach.

## Making Mealtime Pleasant

We all like mealtime to be pleasant. Mealtime arguments
can spoil everyone's appetite. Now is the time, while your

child is small, to start the habit of happy mealtimes. Fussing at your child to get him to eat will get you nowhere.

Most toddlers gain only three to five pounds between 12 and 24 months, and another three to five pounds by age 3. It's important for you to understand this slower growth rate because this means your toddler may not need to eat as much as you think he should.

Toddlers may go through stages when they will eat only a very few foods. It's okay to have a limited diet as long as it's balanced. Try to have something from each of the Basic Four food groups each day. His diet may seem monotonous to you, but that's all right.

Children who are served nutritious food and very little junk food tend to eat when they're hungry. If they aren't hungry, they probably shouldn't eat anyway. So don't nag! Instead, use mealtime to talk about what's happening today.

If it's just you and your child, you can talk about the shape and color of the food, how it was prepared, where milk comes from, and other topics of interest to your child. If other family members are present, conversation won't be so child-centered, but it can still be concerned mostly with the pleasant happenings of the day.

## "Where Do Babies Come From?"

Your toddler may start asking questions about sex. If he does, let him know you appreciate his questions, then answer in terms he can understand. When he asks, "Where do babies come from?" you might say, "Babies grow in a special place in the mother's body."

If he asks how the baby got inside the mother, you can tell him that a mother and a father make a baby together. You might explain that the father's sperm gets into the mother through the father's penis.

Sometimes little girls worry because they have no penis, and little boys worry that their penis might come off.

Explain that boys and girls are made differently. Teach your child the correct names for his/her genitals. Name them as you name other body parts.

All little boys and girls handle their genitals. When they do, and find that this feels good, they may masturbate. This does no harm. It is normal, and you would be wise to ignore it.

A parent who tells his/her child that masturbation is bad may cause the child to feel naughty, or to think that sex or sexual feelings are bad. That's not a very realistic or healthy approach.

## "Don't Talk to Strangers"

Parents often worry about their toddler being molested, especially the parent who was sexually molested when s/he was a child. You certainly don't want this to happen to your child. Neither do you want to teach your child to be afraid of all strangers. Shalimar commented:

> *I tell her not to talk to strangers because some people are bad. One time a man came to our door and she went up and hugged him. I said, "Ellie, you don't hug strangers. If mommy knows him, it's all right." She seemed to understand.*
>
> *I was a victim so I'm very careful. I don't want to make her stay in all the time, but I want her to know there are people who could hurt her. Not everybody is going to hurt her, but some people might.*
>
> Shalimar

A high percentage of molestation is done by someone the child knows and may trust. So how do you help your child prevent this kind of hurt? Melinda had a suggestion:

> *When I give Karena a bath, I say, "These are your private parts and you don't let anybody touch them. If*

*somebody does, please tell mommy. You won't get in trouble, and mommy needs to know."*

*You need to let the child know she can come to her mother for anything. She can tell mother if something bad happens.*

*If kids have secure feelings basically, that's a big protection.*

Melinda, 25 - Sheila, 9; Mathew, 6; Karena, 2

## Potty Training

*He's 25 months old now. Toilet training is one thing that's very difficult right now. He loves wearing training pants, and he says he's a big boy then.*

*He knows why he has to go in the toilet, but he's scared when he has to do #2. For about two days he went pretty good. He'd try so hard, but sometimes he'd start crying. I'd leave him there, and he'd come running and pee on the carpet.*

*Sometimes he goes into the bathroom, and he will say, "Take my diapers down." He will pee with his dad, but he's not ready for #2. Sometimes on the weekends I let him wear his underwear, and he will tell everybody. But if he has to go pee, he will wet his pants.*

Jessica, 17 - Craig, 30 months

This little boy is showing many signs of stress, and his parents are too. He wants to succeed and please his parents, but developmentally he's not quite ready. It would be better to wait a month or two, then try training again. By then he may have developed the ability to hold his urine or release it when he chooses. He may be more able to control his bowl movement (BM) too.

Little boys often train later than little girls. Many are unable to train until they're three or even older. It's a lot less stressful and more productive not to try training until he's developmentally ready.

> *Right after the bottle we bought those little pull-up pants. Before that we would set him down on the little toilet seat in the morning, and he liked that at first. Then he refused to go, so we just kept the diaper on him. Then a little later he started doing it almost on his own.*
>
> Bette, 18 - Kenny, 33 months

Often a child will like to potty train at first. He may enjoy the new training pants or potty chair, but the added attention he's getting probably is more important to him. He may lose interest as training settles into a routine.

Putting him back in diapers, and trying again a month or so later is a good idea. If you can be relaxed about potty training, it will be much easier for everyone.

For a broader discussion of toilet training, see *Teens Parenting—Discipline from Birth to Three.*

## Hard to Accept Change

> *The last couple of days Ellie wants me all the time. She wants to be with me 24 hours a day. Her father left two months ago, and she's happier now, but I think that made her feel a little insecure.*
>
> Shalimar, 19

Ellie may be "happier now" that her father is gone, but at the same time, she undoubtedly misses him. She needs some extra attention from her mother for awhile.

For all kinds of reasons, your child may become more dependent on you at about age two, especially if you have to be separated from him for awhile. It's hard for children of this age to cope with change in their lives. If you must leave your child with a new babysitter, let him have time to adjust to the person before you leave. A big change like dad leaving or even the family moving into a different home may be especially difficult for your toddler.

If you're moving, prepare in advance. Talk to your child about it. As you pack, let him pack some of his toys in a box. You may need to repack them later, but if you let him be a part of the process, it will all seem less strange to him.

Tell him how the furniture and clothing, and especially his toys, will be moved from one place to the other. Explain what your new home will be like, and where he will sleep and play. Let him see it in advance if possible. The more familiar the moving process is to him, the less anxious he is likely to be.

Toddlers are more secure when their life has a predictable routine. They want to sleep in their own bed with a special blanket or stuffed animal. Mom or dad may be the only ones who can put them to bed without tears. The same may be true of eating. They want a predictable routine.

## Even More Patience Needed

While your two-year-old may appear clingy and dependent at times, at other times she will insist on doing things her way:

> *If she gets her mind on something, she'll do it whether I want her to or not. If I want to do her hair, she won't let me do it. She gets in these moods where she won't let anybody touch her. In fact, sometimes she kicks and she screams over almost nothing.*
>
> Shalimar

This can be a difficult time for a toddler. She wants so much to be independent, but simply can't do everything she wants to do. It's best to allow time for her to dress and

*"You can't see me." (Her version of hide and seek.)*

undress herself, and to be available when she can't quite do it alone. At times she will be cooperative, and at other times, extremely unreasonable.

Develop your patience to the fullest. This is not the time to allow yourself the luxury of being impatient. Your toddler needs your help to cope with her moodiness.

> *He doesn't listen to us. He always likes to do his own thing, and he's demanding. He says "No" to everything, and he always asks "Why?"*
>
> Sarah, 17 - Leon, 30 months

Now you need to be especially consistent in your interactions with your child. If you tell her one thing today, you need to follow the same rule tomorrow.

Routine is important for two-year-olds. She likes to do things the same way day after day after day. Her bedtime routine may become even more elaborate.

These are busy months for you and for your toddler. She still has much to learn about her world. If she's given plenty of opportunity to explore, as we've said so often in these books, she'll learn more. She also will keep you alert as you supervise her exploring!

*People say she's spoiled, but I don't let her go too far. She's a kid and they explore and they do things. If you put too many limitations on a child, you never know how much she can learn.*

                                                                    Shalimar

## Winning—For Both of You

Talking about a power struggle between a grownup (you) and your toddler may sound silly. Of course you have the power if we're talking about physical force. If your child won't go to bed, you can pick her up, even if she's kicking and screaming, and put her in her bed.

If you do this, who wins? Certainly not your child. And you don't win either if she's crying and screaming and extremely unhappy.

Try to move inside your toddler's head for a minute. How does she feel? At the same time, think about how you feel. What can you do so you *both* will win?

Time may be a big factor in this kind of stress. You have a great deal to do. If you're in school and/or have a job, you need to get a lot done while you're with your child. It's normal to try to hurry her at mealtime, when she's getting dressed, and when it's time for her to go to bed. As she feels pressured, however, she's likely to dawdle even more. Perhaps she'll declare flatly that she's not going to eat, or go to bed, or get dressed, or whatever it is she must do.

Experiment with taking ten more minutes to get her ready for school. Stretch that bedtime routine a little more. You may find she's more likely to go along with what you want her to do.

Setting a timer might help. For example, show her a timer set for ten minutes. Explain that when the timer dings, lunch will be ready. Toddlers tend to be completely absorbed in their play and dislike being interrupted. They need closure. Advance notice that it's almost time to change activities may help her cooperate.

## You're His Model

*I think it's very very hard being a parent. I don't regret it, but I wish I had waited. Seeing him grow up as a little person is making me think twice before I act because he mimics me and looks up to me. I'm the person he copies, his role model.*

*I used to dip cookies in my milk and he started doing that. My boyfriend said, "If you don't want your son to do that, you can't do it." He was right of course.*

Natalie

Being your child's role model is an awesome responsibility. Observe your child playing with dolls and you're likely to learn how you sound to him. Children whose parents yell a lot often yell at their dolls. It is also true that children whose parents take the time to explain their activities to their child may find him talking in a similar fashion with his "baby."

Toddlers need a lot of attention. They're growing and learning rapidly. Positive attention from significant persons makes the learning seem more meaningful and important.

Watching him learn is exciting for you. Experiencing that learning is even more exciting for your toddler.

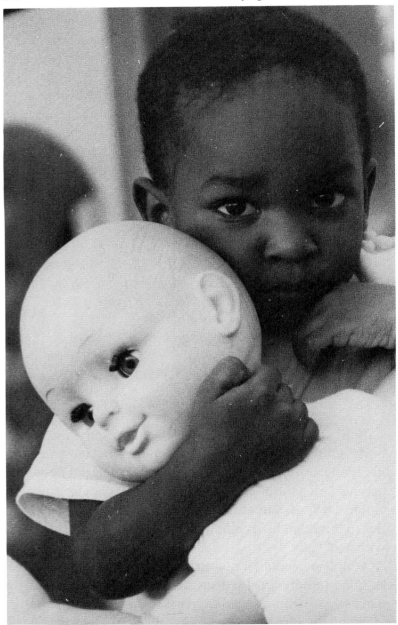

*Many two-year-olds enjoy playing with dolls.*

# Playing With Your Two-Year-Old

*I think this is the best age. You aren't alone. Ellie talks to me, and she understands me more. She gets up and runs. I can play with her. I chase her around. We play hide and go seek, and we play ball. This is more fun for me, and besides, it's not like I'm by myself.*

Shalimar, 19 - Ellie, 30 months

*They can give you a hard time because you have to follow them around, and you have to watch them all the time. Sometimes they make me mad, but they also make me feel happy.*

*Ricardo got my makeup the other day. When we found him, he had lipstick all over his face and black mascara on his forehead. He looked pretty silly!*

Kirsten, 20 - Ricardo, 35 months; Monique, 16 months

Your two-year-old is more self-sufficient now. She can play by herself, but she still loves and needs your attention. If you play with her regularly, she will learn more. She'll also be more willing to play by herself other times.

This doesn't mean you need to spend all your time entertaining her. That wouldn't be good for her either. Some of the time she'll be satisfied to play near you while you do your work.

## Made-at-Home Toys

Even if he owns a lot of toys, your toddler is likely to prefer homemade items much of the time. One of the best toys you can give him is a big box. If you or someone you know buys a new TV or, even better, a refrigerator or other big appliance, save the box.

Your toddler will love going in and out of it. Together you can cut windows and doors in his new house. He can decorate it with crayons or paints. He can pretend it's his home one day, a school house the next. He can hide from you in his house. You'll hear him giggling as you look for him.

He can use a smaller box for a cook stove. Turn the box over and help your toddler draw burners on the bottom. Help him "cook" a snack for the two of you, then "eat" with him.

Encourage him in his pretend play. He may have an imaginary friend. He may even talk to his friend. Imaginary play is a healthy part of growing up.

Do you have a card table you can set up near you? Drape a sheet or blanket over it, and your toddler has a tent or a cave or whatever he wishes. Let his imagination take over.

When you're cleaning out your closets, choose some cast-offs for a dress-up box for your child. He'll like old hats, scarves, mom's or dad's shoes, and other grown-up clothing. Include costume jewelry that's safe for your child—things he can't swallow. Encourage your toddler to pretend he's someone else as he dresses up.

## Plan Painting Time

Take a tip from preschool teachers and do a little organizing of your child's day. Plan a time when she can fingerpaint or paint with a brush. If the weather permits, painting outside cuts back on cleanup time.

Provide plenty of opportunities for your toddler to color, paint, cut paper (with blunt-ended scissors), and other creative activities. You'll continue to supervise, of course:

*In my house the crayons are up in the closet where Mickey can't reach. It's a special time when he can color, or paint, or cut paper. If he wants to cut 100 pieces of paper, that's fine, but he has to do it in a special place.*
Susan, 20 - Mickey, 30 months; Felicia, 11 months

She's not ready to color or paint between the lines in a coloring book. In fact, if she's at all creative, she won't "be ready" later either. Coloring books are a poor investment. Giving her big pieces of paper, then encouraging her to draw or scribble as she thinks best is a far better approach.

*Luke likes to write a lot. I open big paper bags and turn the blank side out. I tape it on the wall, and it's like a big chalk board. He writes all over it. That keeps him busy for a long time.*
Ashley, 18 - Luke, 34 months; Abby, 20 months

Don't worry whether your child uses her left or her right hand. Children often appear to change handedness several times before settling into using one or the other as their "working" hand. Whichever hand she uses is okay. The important thing is not to try to change her preference.

If she's left-handed, she'll be part of the 15 percent of the United States population with this preference. By her third birthday, you'll probably be able to tell whether she is right or left handed.

## Teaching Through Games

You can teach your child colors by talking about the color of his clothes and of other things around him. You can make games by coloring circles of paper various bright colors. Then draw the same size circles on a sheet of paper and color those circles to match the others. Can he match the red cut-out circle with the red circle on the paper?

Does your toddler know his name? If he is separated from you, can he tell someone who he is? You can help him learn by making it a game. Ask him to name family members in photographs, and include photos of him.

Doll play is important to many two-year-olds. If you have another baby now, your toddler may be especially interested in his own baby.

> *Haley has a friend who comes over a lot. They play in the playhouse with their dolls. They change them and talk to them.*
>
> *She'll say, "We're going bye-bye. We have to get ready for school," like I do every morning. One time I heard her say, "Oh-h-h, I'll tell grandma on you."*
>
> Erica, 20 - Haley, 35 months

## Helping Mom and Dad

Pretend play for a two-year-old often means imitating mom or dad.

> *Ricardo wants to do everything I do. When he sees me cooking, he wants to cook. When his dad says he's hungry, Ricardo runs to the kitchen and wants to fix*

*Doll play is important to many two-year-olds.*

*him something. I let him bring the food to his daddy,
and he feels great.*

*Sometimes when I'm washing the dishes Ricardo
wants to help me. I say, "Ricardo, come here and
help me," and he comes running in. He brings his
chair over to the sink and I let him rinse the dishes.*

Kirsten

By the time your child is three years old, he'll be able to
"help" you in many ways. He can set the table, especially if
you provide light-weight plastic dishes. He can help make
his own snack by cutting off a piece of cheese, putting it on
a tortilla, folding over the tortilla, and heating it, with your
help, either in the microwave or the regular oven.

He can help carry in the groceries. He can dust furniture
although you want to be careful about giving him a treated
dust cloth because you don't want him to put it in his
mouth. He can help pick up trash. In fact, he may be
willing to help you do all sorts of things.

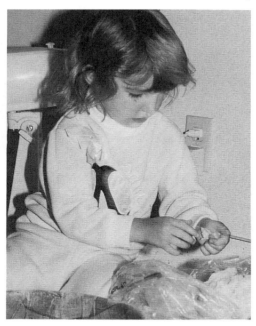

*She's helping make the salad.*

For most children of this age, the magic word is *help*. He probably won't be willing to take on all these jobs simply because you ask him to. His incentive in doing jobs is to be like you.

## Celebrating Holidays

You may be eager to share Halloween with your child. Or you may be looking forward to introducing your toddler to Santa Claus at your local department store. You may find, however, that your little one is not thrilled with either experience.

Santa Claus may scare your toddler because she thinks he's real. He's big and fat, he wears funny clothes, has a peculiar beard, and he sits there and glares at her. She may burst into tears and ruin your photograph.

Halloween scares many toddlers for the same reason. When they're a year old, they may accept whatever is, including witches. By age two or three, they're more likely to be frightened. They don't understand fantasy, and they believe these outlandish characters are real.

To help make these events less frightening, talk to your toddler beforehand about where you're going and what you'll see. Maybe you can practice. Show her pictures of Santa. Play with masks together before Halloween.

When the day arrives, don't rush your child into this new experience. Let her watch other children climbing on Santa's lap. Don't pressure her to follow their lead. She may decide it's okay—or she may not. If she doesn't want to see Santa this year, respect her feelings. Perhaps she'll be ready next year.

## How Much Television?

Research shows that aggressive children tend to watch a lot of violence on television. Research also shows that children who watch too much TV show less imagination in their play and at school than do children who watch less television.

Children can learn important things from television. Can you watch TV with your child and talk with him about what he sees and hears? If the two of you watch an hour or so of carefully selected shows a day, and talk together about it, TV may have a positive influence on your toddler.

A toddler who sits in front of the TV set for several hours each day is not involved in the active play he needs. He's also undoubtedly watching shows inappropriate for him—shows with scary scenes, shows which give a distorted view of relationships between men and women, and other situations which tend to scare or confuse him.

If your family watches a lot of TV, you may have little choice in the number of hours the set is on each day. Probably the best tactic in this case is to find a quiet place where you and your child can play away from TV.

## Playing Outside

Playing outside is important to two-year-olds. If you're lucky enough to have a fenced-in yard, she'll probably spend hours there, especially if you can be with her. Remember that she still needs lots of supervision. If your yard

*She's practicing her balancing skills at the park.*

is not securely fenced, you'll need to be with her constantly when she's outside.

Toddlers love to play in sand, dirt, and mud. Give him spoons, cups, and other sand toys. It's best to keep a sandbox covered when he's not playing in it. This keeps out the cats and dogs who like sand too.

He can paint the garage if you get him a small bucket of water and a paint brush. He'll love playing with a squirt bottle filled with water. By now he may be able to blow soap bubbles.

If you don't have a yard, can you take him to a nearby park often? Taking him for a walk each day will satisfy some of his need to be outside. Of course this won't be the kind of walk where you get lots of exercise from walking rapidly. Your toddler will explore all sorts of things along the way. He'll be in no hurry.

Outings to the airport to watch the planes landing and taking off, to the train station, and to a building site will excite him as much as taking him to Disneyland. Of course, if you're observing a construction site, you and your child will hold hands as you watch.

> *We stop for fire engines. We go to the harbor and watch the boats. Haley points at helicopters going over and says, "Copters."*
>
> *We take her to a petting farm where there are chickens and goats. She likes to pet them. We started going there when she was 2.*
>
> *We also go to the park and feed the ducks.*
>
> Erica

If you live near a beach, you and your toddler may enjoy playing there. Of course you'll be constantly watching her. You also need to be extra careful about sunburn. Most toddlers have sensitive skin and burn easily.

> *She loves the beach. When the waves go out, she runs down there, then runs back when they're coming in. She likes chasing the birds, and she loves to lie in the sand.*
>
> Shalimar

## An Athlete Already?

> *I think Luke's going to be a good baseball player. His dad likes to play baseball with him. When we play, Luke knows how to hold his little plastic bat real good. He hits the ball a lot when we throw it at him.*
>
> Ashley

Lots of fathers and mothers look forward to playing ball with their children. By the time she's two, dad may be playing catch with her. She's not ready for rules yet, but she may thoroughly enjoy playing ball her way with mom or dad.

Leon's parents described his ball-playing mania:

*Glen: Leon watches basketball with me. He knows how to dribble a basketball already. He doesn't like to play with trucks, but he plays with balls constantly.*

*Sarah: When I tell him to throw his clothes in the hamper, he shoots them in, and yells, "Two points!" He watches sports on TV all the time with his dad.*

## How Much Rough-Housing?

Rough-housing is an activity that toddlers and parents, especially dads, often enjoy. It's not smart, however, to play at hitting each other if you don't want your child to hit other children. Neither is it wise to get your child so excited that he'll have trouble calming down.

*I think parents set the pace. My husband likes to play rough. Then he gets tired and wants to stop, but the kids aren't ready to stop. You can't just all of a sudden stop. You have to start going slower and taking it easier. It took him awhile to learn that.*
Annabel, 26 - Andrew, 10; Anthony, 7; Bianca, 5; Brooke, 2

Active play usually is not a good idea at bedtime. You want your child to slow down. That's why a bedtime routine including a story time works best.

## Toddlers and Pets

Toddlers usually enjoy playing with the family dog or cat. The animal must, of course, be extremely gentle and willing to tolerate the child's advances.

*Johnnie has a puppy, and it's something like having a little brother. He feeds the dog when it's time for her to eat. When he wakes up, I ask, "Does the puppy have milk?" and Johnnie feeds her. She's a month old, black and real fluffy with little boots.*

*The puppy treats Johnnie like a little friend. I never
had a pet, and that's why I got him a dog. I wanted
him to have a pet. He makes the little puppy sit down,
and he talks to her. Once he bathed her in dirt.*

Natalie, 17 - Johnnie, 26 months

## What About Cold Weather?

*Susie loves to go outside but it's cold already. She
has to be inside a lot or she'll get sick. We try to
explain, but she's still too little to understand.*

Cathi, 19 - Susie, 34 months

This sounds like a power struggle. Usually a preschool
child can be bundled up warm enough not to get cold when
she's playing outside. Susie is probably quite active while
she's playing and may not feel cold at all.

The mother may have a much bigger problem trying to
stay warm. Cathi may not be dressed as warmly, and she is
undoubtedly less active than her child.

The mother should claim the problem. She should tell
her daughter that she's cold and needs to go back in the
house now to get warm. Together they could work on some
rules for outside play such as the length of time they'll stay
outside. It might help if an indoor play area with room for
active play could be arranged for days when she really
can't go outside.

Toddlers enjoy playing outside. It's good for them. They
are usually more active outside than inside. The exercise
helps their motor development. It also gives them a better
appetite and makes them more ready for bedtime.

The whole world is fantastic to your toddler. Everything
is new. Toddlers really don't need Disneyland because
they can find excitement wherever they are. Your job is to
share his excitement, and to guide and support him as he
discovers his world.

*She needs to hold your hand when she crosses the street.*

# Guarding Your Toddler's Health and Safety

*When William gets in the car, the first thing he does is fasten his seat belt. He's used to it. If I don't fasten mine instantly, he says, "You don't have yours on."*

*I say, "Okay," and I put it on.*

Marlene, 19 - William, 4; Soraya, 18 months

*We're in an apartment, and sometimes there's broken glass on the sidewalk. I pick it up when I see it, but I can't get it all.*

*Madison and Abby like to go barefoot outside. Once Madison stepped on some glass and cut his foot, so now he wears shoes. In hot weather he likes sandals.*

Ashley, 18 - Luke, 34 months; Abby, 20 months

You probably were quite safety conscious during your child's first year. You didn't leave him alone even for a minute on a bed or changing table even though you "knew" he couldn't turn over. You realized how quickly a baby can roll off such a surface.

When your baby started crawling, you may have checked out your home at his eye level. This is a good way to spot the dangers. You probably covered the electric outlets, and perhaps you were able to child-proof your home to a great extent.

## Toddler Needs Even More Supervision

**Mark:** *Dustin likes to climb and he's always getting hurt.*

**Kelly Ellen:** *He has bruises all over his legs.*

**Mark:** *He'll climb on anything. He doesn't cry long when he gets hurt, just briefly. He likes ice on his boo-boos. He tests me when I tell him not to run into the road. Now he stops and doesn't run out there.*

Kelly Ellen, 20, and Mark, 22 - Dustin, 30 months

Your toddler needs even more careful watching than he did a few months earlier. He's running everywhere, but his judgment develops much more slowly. During this sensory motor stage, the steady supervision continues. He has to try things to find out what will happen, yet he's unable to think it through and predict what will really happen. It's your job to keep him safe.

Don't ever leave your baby or toddler alone in your house or apartment—even if he's sleeping. Don't ever leave him alone in your parked car either, even if you're just running into the store for one quick item.

Children left in cars in the summer can die from the heat. There is also the danger the child will lock the doors and not be able to get out in an emergency.

He can probably turn doorknobs and open doors by his second birthday. It's even more important that you keep dangerous things out of his sight and out of his reach.

It's doubly important to keep trash cans securely covered or in a closed-off area when toddlers are running around. A small child can get in lots of trouble by playing in the trash.

Check your home again for hazards. Many toddlers climb amazingly well even before they can walk. Climbing means she can get into even more trouble if you don't watch her constantly.

> *He doesn't know. The whole world is a big adventure, and that's scary. He could fall on something, and he always wants to put things in his mouth. It takes 24 hours of supervision—unless he's sleeping. Then you can finally relax.*
>
> *My grandpa does a lot of watching because when I was little, I almost died when I choked on an apple. He's there watching, watching, being protective. Nathan is really quick and, when he's outside, he can run out in the street so fast.*
>
> Esteban, 19 - Nathan, 28 months; Ralph, 10 months (Priscilla, 17)

## Protect Him from Burns

> *One day I left my curling iron on the bathroom counter. I had turned it off, but it was still hot. Haley went into the bathroom and put her hand on it. She started screaming, "I touched hot. I touched hot."*
>
> *It made a blister, and I put ice on it. The doctor said not to pop the blister, so I didn't.*
>
> Erica, 20 - Haley, 35 months

Toddlers are at great risk for being burned. They can be scalded by pulling a cup of coffee or tea off the table on to themselves. They can be burned by touching a hot stove, iron, or heater. When you're carrying hot food to the table, you must be extremely careful. If your toddler is playing on the floor beside you, you could spill hot food on him.

When he's learning to walk, his ability to reach develops rapidly. The child who was confined to crawling on the floor last week may be pulling himself up by grabbing the table or the stove this week. Hot food, liquids, and heavy items must *not* be left near the edge of the table or stove.

## Poisoning Is Big Danger

Children are most likely to be poisoned when they're ten to twenty months old. They move around a lot, explore everything in reach, put everything possible in their mouths, and aren't able to understand what's dangerous and what's not.

Cigarettes are poisonous. If members of your family smoke, use your best negotiating skills to get them to help keep ash trays out of the reach of your toddler.

The fact that your toddler goes everywhere and explores everything is exciting because you know that's how he's learning. It's also scary because you know how easily he can be hurt. If it's a white powder, he thinks it's sugar. If it's a colored liquid, it must be juice. It may actually be a poisonous perfume or insecticide, but he won't know the difference until he tries it.

> *One time I left a cup of bleach up on the sink. I guess Luke thought it was water and he drank it. I smelled something and I realized the smell came from his mouth. I ran to get my mother. By the time we got back, my husband had put his finger down Luke's throat and made him throw up.*
>
> *Now we don't leave anything like that lying around. We're also careful about small objects because the kids could choke on them.*
>
> Ashley

It's your job to keep your child safe. Check your house, garage and yard often for items that could be dangerous to touch or eat.

Know the plants around your home. Oleander and castor beans, for example, are dangerous if eaten, and can kill a child.

Find the telephone number of your nearest Poison Control Center. Keep it by your phone along with your doctor's and other emergency numbers. If you think your child has been poisoned, take any evidence you have of what he swallowed—a piece of the substance or the container it was in.

Get some syrup of ipecac from your pharmacist and use it *if* your doctor or poison control center recommends it. It will help your child throw up. For some poisons, this is appropriate.

For others, such as toilet and drain cleaners, it's exactly what you *don't* want. Throwing up Drano will cause twice the damage because the lye burns going down and again coming up.

## Cars Can Be Deadly

Cars can be deadly for toddlers. If he's in the car, make sure he's buckled into his car seat. If he weighs 40 pounds or more, he can use the regular seat belt. Incidentally, be just as sure that you're buckled in too. You're his model.

*Going in the street—that's a big one. Right away she thinks she can go in the street. One day she ran out, and here comes a car. I screamed at her and spanked her. Since then, she goes up to the curb, she looks, and then she walks away.*

*I say, "If the ball goes in the street, you come get mommy," and "If your friends cross the street, don't follow them. You come to me and I'll help you."*

*We cross the street together. She's learning. I tell*
*her all the time, "Cars won't see you, Haley," and*
*she'll say, "Okay, Mommy, I'll wait for you."*

Erica

Your toddler moves quickly, but is only now beginning
to develop the ability and self-control to stay out of busy
streets and to watch for cars as he crosses even a garage
driveway.

Insist that he hold your hand when you cross a street, go
through a parking lot, or across a driveway.

For a more detailed discussion of making your home
safe for your toddler, see *Teens Parenting—Your Baby's
First Year.*

## Preventing Serious Illness

Your child should see the doctor for a checkup about
every nine to twelve months during his second and third
years. Before you go to the doctor, write down your questions. It's easy to forget them when you're face to face with
your super-busy doctor.

You've probably made sure your toddler got his DTP
and polio immunizations on schedule during his first year.
When he's 18 months old, he needs to go back for "refills."

At one year he'll need to be immunized against rubella
(German measles), mumps, and red measles. At around the
same time, your doctor may also recommend he receive the
Hib immunization which will protect him from meningitis,
a serious disease in which the lining of the brain becomes
infected. Hib stands for Hemophyllus influenza bacteria.
This is the germ which causes this disease as well as many
ear infections.

The Hib bacteria spreads from person to person. It is
more likely to hit children who attend daycare centers
because they have more contact with other children.

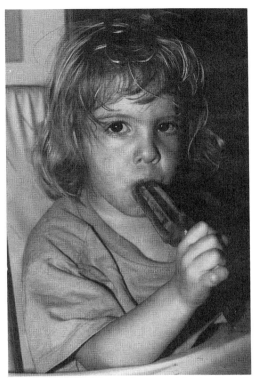

*Eating a popsickle helps provide the liquid she needs if she has a fever or is nauseous.*

## Your Baby Needs a Doctor

If you don't have a doctor for your child, call your local health department. They will give you the name of a doctor and/or tell you of a health department clinic where your child can get a health examination.

Should you have any questions regarding your child's health, be sure to check with your doctor. Write down your observations and questions in advance. They may help your doctor make a diagnosis.

Regular checkups are a good time to ask questions about your child's health and about his growth and development. Talk with your doctor about caring for a sick child at home. Ask what to give for a fever.

How high should your child's temperature be before you call the doctor? Is there a cough syrup to keep on hand? How about allergy medicines?

Your child's vision will be checked as part of his well-baby examination. Any other examinations by eye specialists should be done only if recommended by your pediatrician.

# Diarrhea Still Dangerous

When your child was an infant, you knew how dangerous diarrhea could be. You probably called your doctor
soon after the diarrhea started because you didn't want your
baby to become dehydrated.

Diarrhea is still a dangerous condition for your child.
The dehydration so often associated with diarrhea can be a
serious problem for toddlers too.

The two most important things in caring for the child
with diarrhea are:

• Give lots of liquids.

• Give little or no fat-containing foods such as
  french fries or butter.

# When Your Child Gets Sick

*Haley got strep throat once when I did. She was
about 14 months old, and I was trying to take care of
her by myself. My mom and dad were gone on vaca-
tion, and I was scared and didn't know what to do.
She was feverish, and I kept her in the bathtub for a
long time.*

*Then my aunt came over and said, "You're going
to the doctor." She took us both in, and he prescribed
antibiotics for both of us. That was a terrible week.*

Erica

Doctors often give antibiotics such as penicillin. It is
*very* important to give *all* of the medicine to your child so
the illness doesn't return in a week or two. Sometimes
moms think they can save some medicine to use the next
time the child is sick, but antibiotics don't keep their
strength. If they're used later, they won't help.

Colds are difficult in the preschool years. Attending a
preschool is usually a nice experience for the child, but

unfortunately, she is likely to get many more colds. The first year the child attends any school, this is likely to happen. If the parent waits until she's ready for kindergarten, it will probably happen then.

*He's had a cough when I took him in for his checkup. The doctor said to put the vaporizer on at night, and that seems to help. He's getting better.*
Frederica, 18 - Ricardo, 3½; Raul, 27 months

A cold-water vaporizer is a good investment. Using it in your child's room will help him breathe more easily when he's congested.

Some children have a particularly rough time with asthma and/or allergies:

*Luke gets sick often, mostly coughs and congestion. I think it's allergies. The doctor said it may develop into asthma. They have to give him antibiotics.*

*He got a real high fever once and I put him in the bathtub with cool water. He was crying, but my mom was there to help me.*
Ashley

Having *their* mother's help when their child is sick is very reassuring for many young parents.

For a more detailed discussion on your child's health care, see *Teens Parenting—Your Baby's First Year*.

## Ear Infection Must Be Treated

*Abby had an ear infection last week. I could tell because she's usually a real active baby, but she only wanted to sit on my lap. She was pulling at her ear, and I said, "Abby, does your ear hurt?" She nodded. Of course I took her to the doctor.*
Ashley

If your child appears to have an ear infection, *call the doctor*. Untreated ear infections, in addition to being quite painful, can easily cause loss of hearing. A child who can't hear well misses out on a lot, and is likely to have a difficult time when he starts school.

If he can't hear, he will have a hard time learning to talk. He won't hear how words should sound since he won't be hearing them. His language will sound garbled and be hard to understand. Most ear infections, if caught soon enough, can be treated with no lasting problem.

> *Ellie had a lot of ear infections that first year. Then we realized she wasn't talking, and our friends' babies were talking a lot. We took her to an ear, nose and throat doctor and he said, "She can't hear."*
>
> *We sat in a room where a little monkey rang a bell. Ellie wouldn't even look when he rang the bell.*
>
> *I felt so bad when I found out she was deaf. We had yelled at her, "Ellie, come here," and she wouldn't respond. Then we'd get mad at her.*
>
> *They did surgery on her ears and she's hearing fine now. Two days after the surgery I said, "Ellie," and she looked at me. A couple of days later she was saying "Mommy" for the first time. She also likes music now. She couldn't hear it before.*
>
> Shalimar, 19 - Ellie, 30 months

## Care for Toddlers' Teeth

Your toddler may have had no trouble cutting his early teeth. His first and second molars, which come through during his second year, can be a different matter. He may be quite miserable and irritable when these molars are coming through his gums.

There isn't much you can do to help other than giving him something cold to bite on. He may like to play with ice cubes. Even rubbing his gums with your finger may help, if only to let him know you're trying to do something for him.

If he seems to be in a lot of pain, it may not be his teeth. If he keeps putting his hand up to the side of his face, perhaps he has an earache. Check with his doctor.

Your toddler needs his own toothbrush. You should be brushing his teeth as soon as three or four teeth have erupted. Now he will want to help, but be sure his teeth are brushed thoroughly at least twice a day.

The easiest way to show him how to brush is to stand him in front of you with the back of his head against you. Brace his head against one hand and brush with the other. Show him how to brush the upper teeth down and the lower teeth up, the way they grow. You'll need to supervise his brushing for several years yet.

Those baby teeth have three important uses:
• They help him move from only milk to solid foods he can chew.
• Baby teeth help shape the child's jaw.
• They help him pronounce words correctly.

For these reasons, you need to take your toddler in for a dental checkup by age 3. If there are cavities, it's important to have them filled.

Keeping your child safe and healthy during her toddler years is an important part of your parenting career. It's up to you to create a safe environment for her. It's up to you to care for her when she's ill. It's also up to you to guide her toward eating the good foods and getting the rest she needs for optimal health.

As you already know, parenting provides lots of challenges. Your reward for meeting these challenges is your child's well-being and love.

*A satisfying partnership takes lots of love, respect, and caring.*

# CHAPTER 12

# The Partnership Challenge

*Being married so young is very stressful. Those first two years were so hard we sometimes thought we were going crazy and wondered if we did the right thing. We have never gone on a big trip or done anything real crazy together due to getting married so early. Money is very tight.*

*I would love to go back to school and get a BA degree, but I can't because of the money. My parents will pay for my schooling, but that doesn't cover the rent. By the time I come home, it's too late for night school. I will go some day. I'm waiting patiently.*

Susan, 20 - Mickey, 30 months; Felicia, 11 months

Many teenage mothers are rearing their toddlers alone. The baby's father may have vanished when he learned the young woman was pregnant. Or they may have stayed together throughout pregnancy, perhaps longer, then ended their relationship.

If you're parenting alone, you're probably working very hard and, if you're like many other single parents, you'd rather be sharing your parenting responsibilities.

---

*Making good decisions concerning partners is perhaps one of the hardest issues faced by teenage parents.*

---

If you're with your baby's other parent, however, you probably face some problems in parenting together. If your partner is not your child's other parent, you're also likely to encounter difficulties. Good relationships take time and effort in addition to love just as good parenting takes time and effort in addition to lots of love.

It's hard to parent alone, but it's also difficult to fit in enough time and effort for both your partner and your child. Making good decisions concerning partners is perhaps one of the hardest issues faced by teenage parents. There is likely to be even more heartbreak in a failed relationship when there is a child involved.

Teenage parents of toddlers are involved in a variety of relationships. Only one in three teenage mothers is married when her child is born. By the time the child is three, a high percentage of these marriages have ended. By this time, many teenage parents are with a different partner.

## When You Date Again

Sometimes a single teenage mother may wonder if she will ever date again. If a man knows she has a child, will he ask her out? Or will she be left alone to parent her child? Elysha is typical of many teen mothers who say this isn't a problem for them:

*My having a child doesn't bother anyone. I had thought a lot of young men would think, "Well, you have a child so I won't bother." But a lot of the guys I know are attached to Antoine.*

*"Can Antoine come with us?" they ask. Sometimes we include him.*

*The only time I date are the weekends. I work eight hours a day, then pick up my child at school. We do what we have to do at home, we go to bed, and then we start the day again.*

Elysha, 22 - Antoine, 4

Sometimes it's hard for a toddler to understand why mom leaves her to go out with her boyfriend:

*When a boyfriend comes to pick me up, Susie decides she wants to go. She puts her clothes on and follows me out to the car. We try to explain, "Mommy is going out, and you have to stay home."*

*My mom usually picks Susie up and brings her in the house. She cries until she realizes mom will come home later. Then she goes to bed.*

Cathi, 18 - Susie, 34 months

If Cathi talked with Susie ahead of time about her plans for the evening, Susie might be more accepting. Perhaps Cathi could do something special with Susie before she goes out. If Cathi's date means she won't be able to read Susie a bedtime story, perhaps they could have a reading session earlier in the day.

Shalimar is pleased that her friend Pete makes a special effort to include Ellie in their plans:

*It makes me feel better, because if Ellie didn't like the person I'm dating, I'd have a problem.*

*The first time she saw Pete kiss me, she said, "Don't kiss my mom."*

*Pete said, "Ellie, I love your mom too. I like both
you and your mom, and I want to be with you both."
Then he gave her a hug goodbye, and she kissed him.*

Shalimar, 19 - Ellie, 30 months

## Is Marriage a Solution?

Some parenting couples stay together, but choose not to
marry during pregnancy, or perhaps not for months or even
years after their baby is born. Many of these young couples
live together. At first, they are likely to be with his parents
or hers because they can't afford a place of their own. By
the time their child is a toddler, they may have their own
apartment.

Sometimes a teenager's parents push her into marriage
after she has become pregnant. This happened to
Rosemarie.

Rosemarie is fairly typical of many young mothers who
rush into marriage. She and Dick struggled for two years to
make their marriage work, but their relationship steadily
grew worse:

*I got married because I was pregnant. My parents
forced us into it. It was the wrong reason, but my
mom seemed to think it was the solution. We told them
on Monday night that I was pregnant. By Saturday,
we were in Las Vegas getting married.*

*We were both back in school on Monday morning.
We were living with my parents—stayed with them
that whole first year. That was a hard way to start a
marriage. They were very supportive, and actually
helped us financially for awhile.*

*However, they treated us like the high school kids
we were. They wanted to know where we were going
whenever we went out, what time we'd be back, the
whole thing.*

*We graduated from high school a year after Helen was born. We both found jobs, and my mother-in-law took care of Helen. We rented a little apartment not far from my folks' house.*

Rosemarie, 19 - Helen, 3

Like many other teenage couples, Rosemarie and Dick thought moving out on their own would solve their problems. This didn't happen:

*Moving out didn't solve our problems. We were fighting more and more.*

*Then one day Dick hit me, and that did it. My father used to knock us around when I was little, and I vowed that when I grew up, nobody was going to hit me. I had warned Dick I'd leave if he ever hit me. So I did.*

Sadly, violence is a part of many teenage (and older) relationships. It takes a great deal of courage for a woman to walk out of such a relationship, especially if she has no money and no place to go. Rosemarie at least had a high school education and some job skills. She continued her story:

*To be perfectly honest, right after my divorce, I didn't know how we would survive. But I didn't have a choice. I couldn't live with him. Now I'm trying to put my life back together, and I'm adjusting pretty well.*

*Helen and I are living with my sister and her husband and their baby. We can't afford a decent apartment by ourselves, so I split living expenses with them. I couldn't handle living with my parents now because they would try to take over. Being with my sister is a little different because we're peers.*

Rosemarie

If you're in an abusive relationship, do everything you can to get out of it. *You don't deserve to be hit!*

Check the phone book or ask your school counselor or your social worker for information about women's shelters in your area, shelters which take women and children. You might find reading *Say "No!" to Violence* by Mary Maracek helpful. (See Appendix.) Included are vignettes of women in abusive relationships together with suggestions for escaping such a relationship.

## Divorce Is Difficult

For some married couples, divorce may be the best solution to a lot of unhappiness. Divorce is usually not easy, however.

Cara and Cliff were married before Leroy was born, and they had two more children within three years. When Nicole was two, they divorced. Cara commented:

> *You have to adjust all over when you divorce. If I hadn't been married, I wouldn't have to go through this. I think it's harder because I was used to having somebody here. I can't even go to the store by myself now.*
>
> *I've been to a lot of counseling. The counselor made me realize this is the way it's going to be, and I have to deal with it. I can't go around it. It's real, and I have to deal with it.*
>
> Cara, 24 - Leroy, 8; Paul, 6; Nicole, 5

Sometimes marriage counseling *before* divorce can help a couple work through their problems. Divorce is seldom easy for either partner, and it's almost always hard on the children involved.

Divorce doesn't solve problems. It's the people involved who must solve those problems. For some, divorce may be a necessary step, but it won't be easy.

# Back Together After Six-Month Separation

When a couple separates, it's not always permanent. Sometimes a few months of living apart helps both partners realize more clearly the positive side of their relationship. This was the case with Angelica and Cody.

When Angelica was 17, she and Cody wanted to be married. They weren't yet pregnant, and Angelica's mother said they were too young. The young couple decided to push the issue:

> *Sharon was planned. I wanted to be married. My mom wouldn't sign because I was 17, so we decided to get pregnant. Then she signed.*
>
> *We lived with his parents for three months because we were saving to buy a house. We moved into a house in November. It was hard. I didn't realize all the financial things, the house payments, everything. It's a lot different when you own than when you rent.*

Because there wasn't enough money and because of Cody's involvement in drugs, the young couple separated for six months when Sharon was 2. Angelica continued:

> *We were separated about 6 months, and our divorce was almost final. At that time I wasn't doing drugs or anything, and he got worse after I left. It was hard going back to my mom and dad. They paid the down payment for the lawyer, and it was difficult to ask for that. All along, his family thought I was leaving because of money. I didn't want to bring out the drugs and all the bad things.*

Cody finally got help with his drug problem, and now he's staying clean. He and Angelica have been back together for a year. Looking back, Angelica is convinced the separation served a purpose:

*Yes, it helped our relationship for me to be on my own for awhile. We were having a lot of financial problems, house payments, car payments. We charged everything we could. That was very stressful for me. I gained a lot of weight. I was working more hours than Cody, and he would skip work because he didn't feel like going. That was hurting me because I was working so hard to make ends meet while he didn't seem to care.*

*I felt Cody didn't care about me and my job. I think when we separated, he realized I wasn't just there. I think he had been taking me for granted. When I was gone he realized how much I was doing.*

Angelica credits Sharon with reuniting her parents:

*When we separated, I started seeing the things I missed. The main reason I went back was Sharon. Each time Cody and I were together she didn't want us to separate. At first we'd fight.*

*Then we started doing things together because of Sharon, and then we started liking to be together again. And dating wasn't that easy. It was hard. It was hard to be single.*

*I had bills to pay, car insurance. It was real hard with a $4.50 an hour job, and I absolutely couldn't get anything else.*

*Recently Cody, Sharon, and I went to Sea World together, and we had a wonderful time. I'm glad we're back together.*

Angelica, 20 - Sharon, 3

## Marriage Can Work

Marriage, of course, works well for some teenage couples. Tamera hadn't planned to marry so soon. But she loves her children and her husband, and she's satisfied with her life now. She knows that if she starts preparing herself soon, she can still have the career she wanted. It will be a little delayed, but it will happen:

*Early marriage—it's hard. Sometimes I wish I had waited. There are a lot of things I missed out on. But I wouldn't give up my kids for anything because right now they are my whole life.*

*I figure that since I didn't get to do a lot of things when I was a teenager, I'll be quite young when they're in their teens. Then I can be independent and do things I want to do but can't now.*

*This September Curt and I are going to start taking night classes at college. I may take accounting. I won't rush right into it, but over a little while I'll start getting my education so I can have a career.*

*Then I can get a good-paying job when the kids are older. When they're teenagers, I can go out and have my career, and it won't interfere with them. Curt thinks that is super-fantastic.*

Tamera, 21 - DeeDee, 4; Leon, 20 months

If you're married already, you're probably trying hard to make it work. Good luck and best wishes!

---

*Work hard together to make your marriage a happy and satisfying long-term relationship.*

---

If you're thinking of getting married, make your decision very carefully. If you both are absolutely certain marriage to each other is right for both of you, get married. Then work hard together to make your marriage a happy and satisfying long-term relationship.

## Making the Marriage Decision

Whether you've never been married, or you're divorced, you may be considering marriage now. If you are, you and your partner may want to discuss such things as:

- Do you both want to spend *all* the rest of your life together?
- Is one of you working and earning enough to support your family? If only one is working, is s/he willing to support the other one and your child?
- Do you have a place to live? For most couples, it's harder to develop a good relationship while you're living with other people.
- Do your answers agree on such important questions as:
    - When will you have your next child?
    - Will either or both of you continue going to school?
    - Who is expected to have a job? Husband? Wife? Both?
    - Who will take primary responsibility for the care of your child?

You can think of a lot of other things you need to discuss thoroughly before you decide to spend the rest of your lives together.

The two of you might like to read *Teenage Marriage: Coping with Reality* together. You'll find a lot of suggestions for making a partnership work, whether you're married or simply living with your partner.

At the back of *Teenage Marriage* is a "Score Card" for teenage marriage decisions. You'll also find a fairly long questionnaire concerning attitudes toward marriage and living together. You and your partner might each like to take this "test," then compare your answers. It might help you see more clearly the areas in which you agree and those in which you disagree.

Completing the questionnaire together is also an excellent way to help you start talking about some important issues. Too often, partners don't communicate well about money, children, families, home preferences, career goals, and other vitally important topics.

## Making a Good Partnership Better

The relationship with your partner may be more complicated because you're a parent. If it's a poor relationship, you may, because of your child, not feel free to leave. If your partner is not your child's father, you may worry about the effect this situation will have on your toddler.

If you're with a partner, you probably would like your relationship to be as good as possible. One thing to remember is that it's important that neither partner feel put down or badly treated by the other.

Sometimes people talk about a good relationship being a 50-50 situation—each partner has equal rights and responsibilities. A better percentage is probably 60-60—each partner goes *more* than half way to please the other. At the same time, each partner needs to realize how important s/he is, and be willing to guard his/her own self-esteen while doing more than his/her share in maintaining a loving and caring relationship with the partner.

Maintaining a good relationship is not easy. It takes a lot of nurturing, but, for many, it is worth the effort.

Living within a good partnership can make parenting even more satisfying.

*Both you and your child are more likely to have the life you want
if you don't have your second child too quickly.*

# CHAPTER 13

# Planning Your Family

*I wish I had had them at least a year further apart. It's hard because Crystal still needs a lot of attention, and Sylvia needs so much, too, with feeding, changing, bathing, and everything else. They need so much, and their father takes a lot of time, too. It's hard trying to divide myself three ways.*

*I used to be able to do what I wanted, but no more. I know I've missed a lot—I feel like I went from being a child to being a mother—and that's exactly what I did.*

Carrie, 18 - Crystal 31 months; Sylvia, 14 months

A lot of teenagers who have one child have another within one or two years. Often this second pregnancy is not planned. It may, in fact, create a real hardship for the young mother:

*I didn't want Kerry—it was a total accident. I was on the pill, but I ran out and was going to wait until after my period. This pregnancy upset me terribly. Amy was the only one I wanted. I don't like having two kids. I thought about abortion, but I knew deep down I wouldn't do it.*

*Her father's mom said, "But that's my first grandchild," and my mom said, "You won't be welcome in the family if you do that." That's my whole family.*
                                            Leslie, 20 - Amy, 27 months; Kerry, 4 months

Sometimes a young woman feels she's ready to be a stay-at-home partner and mother. She's enjoying the child she has, and figures it will be okay to have another right away. Darla totally disagrees with this kind of thinking:

*Girls often think they're completely in love right away, and their boyfriends think they should stay home. It's like playing the part, then realizing later that's not what they want. A lot of girls I know don't go on birth control—at least they end up getting pregnant again. I think they just don't worry about it.*

## Being 17 and having two kids a year apart seems insane to me.

*They may use birth control for awhile, then they go off it. They don't take it seriously. They don't seem to think it will happen again. Being 17 and having two kids a year apart seems insane to me. There are so many things you still have to learn to know what you want. To end up having to teach two kids is too much.*
                                            Darla, 17 - Janis, 2

Darla is outspoken about her ideas on responsibility, birth control, and independence:

*If you want to be an independent person, you can't depend on the man to use birth control. Independence is important to me—it always has been. If you use birth control yourself, you know for sure.*

Darla

Shirley, too, thinks that young mothers who are sexually active should find and *always* use a reliable birth control method:

*Once you're pregnant, it's up to you if you have an abortion or keep it. I don't put anybody down for an abortion, because if you know you won't be happy with that child, it's even more tragic to try to raise it.*

---

## With two or three children and no husband, I'd be really limited.

---

*After she has her baby, every girl should find a birth control method. I think if I get pregnant again, it will be because I want to. If you're in a relationship with one person, both of you should take the responsibility.*

*With one child, I can go ahead and do what I want. With two or three children and no husband, I'd be really limited. I don't want another child until I'm married.*

Shirley, 20 - Virginia, 4

## What Are Your Options?

If you aren't pregnant now, you have three options as far as pregnancy is concerned.

One is obvious. If you don't have sex, you won't get pregnant. The majority of high school students still choose this method. When you see statistics stating that 25 percent of all 15-year-old girls have had sexual intercourse, that means that 75 percent have not.

Your second option is to use birth control if you're having sexual intercourse. If you don't want another baby, this is essential.

> *I have a girlfriend who doesn't use birth control because she says she can't talk about it with her boyfriend. I tell her if she's too embarrassed to talk to him, don't have sex with him. The whole idea is just silly.*
>
> Melinda, 15 - Robin, 9 months

Lots of teenagers think, "It won't happen to me. I won't get pregnant." But one couple in 25 will become pregnant at the time of *first* intercourse. Of the couples having intercourse twelve times without using contraception, *one-half* will become pregnant.

Would you ride in a car if you knew that one-half of those who take twelve rides will have a serious accident? If you aren't ready to have a baby, or if you already have one and aren't ready for another, an unplanned pregnancy is certainly a "serious accident."

Erin and Brian are determined to wait until Alex is older before even considering another pregnancy. Both understand clearly that spacing their babies is up to them:

> *Another baby? Sometimes I think I don't ever want any more. I want to raise him, and by the time he's 20, I'll still be young. Then I can go out and do my own thing.*
>
> *Sometimes, though, I look at him, and I know he would love a little brother or sister, he would love it. Sometimes I say I want another baby, and then I stop and think about all the work it takes. Chris says he wants to wait about three years.*

*After I had the baby, Chris wanted to use two condoms in case one broke! We're really into it. I'm not taking the pill, but we always use the condom and gel.*

*Neither of us will do anything if we don't have protection. Either one of us will say "Do you have a condom? Gel?"*

---

## If the girl doesn't say anything, he assumes she's on the pill.

---

*I think it has to do with both people. Some of the girls will break up with the father and will be with someone else. Either the guy doesn't care, or he will carry something, but if the girl doesn't say anything, he assumes she's on the pill.*

*If you're 15 I don't think there is any reason to have another baby. I don't think it's an accident. The baby is the one that suffers. I don't think a lot of teen parents think about what happens later.*

Erin, 16 - Alex, 12 months

You'll find a description of the various methods of birth control in *Teens Parenting—Your Pregnancy and Newborn Journey*.

Your third option is to get pregnant. If you're having sex and you don't use birth control, this is the option you apparently have chosen.

If you're pregnant now, you still have two options other than raising the child yourself. You can get an abortion, or you can release your child for adoption.

Releasing her child for adoption used to be the accepted "solution" for a pregnant teenager who was not married. Today, however, only four percent of unmarried pregnant adolescents choose adoption for their child. Yet this could

be the most loving, caring decision a birthmother
could make.

For more information on adoption and for personal
accounts of young mothers who chose this option, see
*Pregnant Too Soon: Adoption is an Option.*

## Enough Time for First Child

Many young mothers and fathers want to have enough
time between their babies to give each child the love and
attention he needs. They also realize the expense of having
one child, and prefer to wait at least two or three years
before having another baby.

Kelly Ellen and Mark are married and appear to be
having a wonderful time parenting Dustin. Mark works
full-time while Kelly Ellen goes to school and works part-
time. They discussed possible timing for their next baby:

**Kelly Ellen:** *Another child? Maybe when he's 5.
Everyone is pushing me to have another one now.*

**Mark:** *A lot of the family want us to have another
baby. But we want to get a little more settled in.*

**Kelly Ellen:** *I want to finish school. I want to get
that done before I have another baby.*

**Mark:** *I think we would be well off when she's
working either in the office or as an instructor. If she
were to get pregnant now, we would make do. But I
think it's good to plan like that.*

*I have heard that if you wait for your second child,
perhaps 3 or 4 years, the first child, instead of being
jealous, will love the new baby. I love to give Dustin
attention.*

**Kelly Ellen:** *He's our world. He's the center. He's
the first grandchild and everybody adores him.*

Kelly Ellen, 20, and Mark, 22 - Dustin, 30 months

# Jealous of New Baby

Often, a small child is quite jealous of a new baby. He feels displaced by this new person who takes so much of mom's and dad's attention. Why should he be thrilled? He can't play with the baby. The baby only cries and sleeps. Mom may always seem to be holding the baby instead of him. If the baby finally goes to sleep, mom

*He's less likely to be jealous if he's past the toddler stage.*

may need to sleep too. No wonder the displaced toddler
often feels resentment:

> *Ricardo is jealous of Monique because she's*
> *younger. If we hug Monique, he wants to be hugged*
> *too. When I'm talking to Monique, he will move*
> *between us because he wants attention.*
>
> *When Monique was born he was jealous. He had a*
> *time when he cried so much. Almost anything would*
> *get him to crying. I think it was because of Monique.*
> *He still wants everything that Monique gets.*
> Sharon, 19 - Ricardo, 35 months; Monique, 16 months

Rashion observed the jealousy Athenea felt when
Enrique was born:

> *It's hard having a small child, then having another,*
> *and trying to take care of both. You have to be very*
> *stable, and you have to have a strict budget.*
>
> *There was a lot of jealousy when Enrique was*
> *born. I would tell Athenea this is not only my child.*
> *This is our baby, and we have to take care of this*
> *baby together.*
>
> *That helped a lot because she stopped seeing*
> *Enrique as her brother, and instead as her baby. I'd*
> *let her hold the baby, and I'd show her how.*
> Rashion, 20 - Athenea, 3; Enrique, 22 months

## Planning Helps Parents and Child

Mary, whose second child was not planned, offered good
advice:

> *I was planning to wait even longer to have a baby*
> *although I wanted another one sometime. If things*
> *aren't working out with you and the guy though, don't*
> *just have a baby because you want one. You need to*
> *know two things before you have another baby. Is that*

*father going to be around? Are you going to be able to support the baby?*

*You need to think about lots of things—Do you have a suitable job? Are you planning to go back to school?*

---

## You can't be selfish and have a kid just because you want one.

---

*If you stay home, it's the kids who suffer if you can't support them. You can't provide the clothing, the food, the schooling they need. Having a kid costs a lot of money.*

*You can't be selfish and have a kid just because you want one. It's best to wait until you have a career, even though that's not what I did. If you're settled in a career, you can be sure you can give this child what it needs.*

*My husband and I split six months ago, and I don't even want to think about relationships or commitment at this point. I don't want to rush it. I know that's not the way to handle it.*

Mary, 21 - Shawna, 4; Ahmud, 20 months

There are many reasons to delay your second baby—practical reasons like how will you afford another child? One of the most caring reasons is that you want to have enough time and energy to give your first child the attention he needs. Many young parents feel a toddler is better off being an only child for at least two or three years.

Parenting a child or several children is a wonderful experience. It will be more wonderful if you have the resources—time, money, relationship—that you need to parent well. *Your child and your future children will thank you.*

*Graduating is an important gift to yourself and your child.*

# CHAPTER 14

# Your Future—
# Your Child's Future

*I feel old compared to when I was first pregnant. I look at life differently. I have two children, so I can't just go around not knowing what I want to do with my life. I'm more responsible now, and every minute counts.*

*I work and I go to school. I'm not influenced by my friends like I used to be. Some people, even though they have children, go on with their lives as if their parents are going to take care of the child.*

*It doesn't work that way with me. On both sides our parents don't take the responsibility of raising our kids. I think it's good they don't. If they did, I would be taking it for granted and leaving them with my parents all the time.*

Mary, 21 - Shawna, 4; Ahmud, 20 months

*I stayed in school. You got to go to school so you can get the kind of job you want. I'm not on welfare— I never was. When paycheck time comes around, I'm out of money, but I'm getting there. It's being independent that counts.*

*I want to be an administrative secretary, so I'll be going to junior college for the next two years.*

Ginger, 18 - Sean, 17 months

## Looking Ahead

Your child may be three soon. What kind of future are you planning for him and for yourself? If you're with his father, are you following your dreams of a satisfying life together? Are you already an independent family, or on your way to becoming independent?

If you're by yourself or with another partner, what are your plans for your future? Are you able to support your child if you need to do so? If you aren't to that point, what are you doing now to get there? Are you still in school? Are you learning job skills? Whether you're your child's mother or father, it's essential that you be able to support yourself and your child.

*Even if she's married, the girl should get a job and learn to be independent—especially the way so many are getting divorced today. If she never knew any-thing, dropped out of school because she got preg-nant, and got married, the only thing she's learning is cleaning and cooking. Beyond that, she doesn't know much if she doesn't ever get a job.*

*A lot of kids think they have to marry because they're pregnant, but that's a bunch of nonsense.*

*I didn't feel good about myself at first when I knew I was pregnant. Later, I thought of the way I was, and I decided I didn't want Janis to grow up the way I did.*

*I had to change a lot of my attitudes and think what I
wanted to do to change myself.*

*So often the mother is going to support the child. I
like to work because it makes me feel more independent. I don't have to rely on anybody else.*

Darla, 17 - Janis, 2

## Taking Financial Responsibility

Some teenage fathers and mothers aren't supporting their
child because they're still in school. Others have dropped
out, but can't find a good job. The best approach for them
is to stay in or go back to school and/or get job training to
prepare themselves for supporting their family.

Julio had a low-paying job and, like many young fathers,
wondered how he could possibly support his family:

*I was working a construction job, making just a
little over minimum wage. I thought, "Here we are,
bringing a child into the world, and I'm going to have
to support the child." I told the construction crew I
was going to be a dad, and I wanted some advice.*

*"Leave now," they told me.*

*And "Get an abortion."*

*I hung in there, and when Francene was born, we
had benefits so the medical bills were paid. But so
much else was on my mind. Will I be able to afford
food? The bills? The responsibilities never end.*

*I was worried about being a father. How do you
fill a father's shoes, someone who's supposed to have
all the answers? How do you live up to a father's
reputation?*

Julio, 24 - Francene, 4; Alina, 3; Gloria, 1 (Joanne, 22)

Whether you're the mother or the father, you need to live
up to a parenting "reputation," as Julio says. You'll never
have all the answers—none of us do—but you'll need to be

responsible for your child. Being responsible includes
being financially responsible.

## Fewer Graduates Need Welfare

Women who achieve at least a high school education are
only half as likely to live in households receiving AFDC
(Aid to Families with Dependent Children) as are women
who never graduated.

If the young mother depends on welfare payments, there
is never enough money:

> *Sometimes I run out of money. There is no way I
> can rely on welfare. I work part-time, and my mom
> watches the kids when I work.*
>
> *My cousin said, "I'm going to get pregnant and get
> on welfare." I told her she was crazy.*
>
> *When you move into a new place here in Califor-
> nia, it costs about $1500. They won't rent to you
> unless you're 18, and your parent has to sign for you
> even then. My girlfriend lives with me. She says every
> time she wants a child, she'll take care of one of mine.*
>
> Leslie, 20 - Amy, 27 months; Kerry, 4 months

Candi is determined not to depend on welfare for
financial support:

> *I'm getting ready to get off welfare although I'll
> still get MediCal. I don't need welfare. The sooner I
> get off, the better.*

---

### Now that I'm working and back in school, I feel better about me.

---

> *You get lazy. I got lazy. I didn't want to work. I
> didn't want to go to school. It's better spending
> money I've earned. I hated it when I lived off welfare.*

> *Now that I'm working and I'm back in school, I feel better about me.*
>
> Candi, 16 - Janet, 18 months

Sharon, too, decided to return to school:

> *I'd been out of school for two years. I saw something at the store about this school for teen parents. I wrote down the number, went home, and called. I'm back in school now, and they take care of my kids.*
>
> *I need an education for my kids so I can get a good job. If my kids want to ask me something, I want to be able to answer them. I want the best for them. My husband wants me in school too.*
>
> Sharon, 19 - Ricardo, 35 months; Monique, 16 months

Sharon is lucky. She lives in a school district which provides childcare for students' infants and toddlers.

If your school doesn't have a childcare center, and you don't have a relative or friend who will care for your child while you continue school, what will you do? See *Teens Parenting—Your Baby's First Year* for tips on choosing suitable daycare for your child and suggestions on handling the expense of that care.

## After High School, What?

Often it's important not to put off getting your education. If you've already graduated from high school, you may decide to go ahead with further training as soon as possible.

Shirley graduated from high school three years ago when Virginia was fourteen months old. Because she had learned office skills in high school, Shirley started working for the county in the welfare department a few months later.

After working directly with people applying for welfare, she has some firm opinions on the subject:

*You don't get anywhere on welfare. I hear people*
*saying, "I have these two children who are starving*
*and. . ." All I can say is if you care for yourself as a*
*person and for those children, you'll go out there and*
*work. I could never get what I want waiting for a*
*check on the first and the fifteenth—I couldn't live off*
*what somebody else gives me just because I have a*
*baby. I want a lot of things for me and my daughter.*

Shirley

Remember, if you complete high school, your chances of
being on welfare are half what they are if you drop out
before you graduate.

Parents, fathers as well as mothers, who continue their
education and hold good jobs obviously are much better off
than are parents who quit school and whose only income is
their AFDC grant.

*First I want to get my GED and start moving on,*
*then train with computers. I worry about the future a*
*little. I don't want to be real old and still making*
*minimum wage. I want to be financially secure.*

Miguel, 20 - Genevieve, 18 months (Maurine, 16)

## Job Helps Self-Esteem

Many young parents also discussed the difference a job
can make in the way they feel about themselves. They often
mentioned that when a mother thinks well of herself, when
she has good self-esteem, she's a better mother than she is
when she's unhappy with herself.

*When Martha was little, we stayed by ourselves for*
*almost a year. I was home most of the time, watching*
*TV and being bored. At that time, I wasn't helping*
*myself. I was depending on my parents plus welfare.*

*Now I'm self-supporting. I feel good about myself
because I'm doing it on my own. I've found out I can
cope, and I love my job. I'm a nurse's assistant, and
I'm taking a medical terminology class.*

*I think I'm a better mother when I like myself.*

Alta, 22 - Martha, 6; Howard, 3

Carla, unlike many young mothers, can afford to stay
home with her children now because her husband earns
enough to support the family. She, too, however, understands the importance of continuing her education:

*I know the kids are going to grow up, and I don't
want to sit home all the time. I love doing what I'm
doing now, but they won't be this little forever. I want
to have something for myself.*

*I'm going back to school one night a week this fall.
Norm is pleased that I am.*

*When I see a young mother sitting home alone with
her kids, doing nothing but waiting on them and her
husband, I feel like saying, "Don't sit home, being
bored and getting fat. Your husband won't like you
any more—and neither will you like yourself."*

Celia, 21 - Laurel, 4 years; Lance, 18 months

Have you already dropped out of school? Now, this
minute, is the time to return. You can go back to your
regular school or to a special class for teen parents. In most
states, if you're 18 or older, you can go to a local community college to take classes to help you earn your high
school diploma.

Check community college catalogs for job training
facilities. Possibilities may include Regional Occupation
Programs (ROP) and high school career centers. You may
find help with childcare or transportation, especially if
you're receiving welfare. Talk to your social worker.

## Who Stays Home with the Kids?

If you're with a partner, both of you may need to work simply to be able to pay your bills. Or one of you may decide to stay home with your child(ren) while the other one keeps a job.

In traditional families, the mother stays home and takes care of the children and cleans the house. If they can afford it, many families still prefer to have a parent home while the children are tiny. Either the mother or the father can care for the children, and either the mother or father can support the family. More often today, however, parents share both roles.

## Heavy Expense of Moving Out

Living with your own parents is often difficult when you have a child yourself. Wanting to move into a place of one's own is certainly an understandable goal. If you've never lived on your own, if your parents have always paid the bills, you may not realize how expensive it is to keep an apartment.

*I plan to move out in three months when Holly (friend with a baby) turns 18. I'm 16. Hopefully I can get $350 from welfare. An apartment will be $500 a month, and I'll split that with Holly. Then we can go half on the groceries, and Robin will be eating table food by then. We should be able to make it.*

Melinda, 16 - Robin, 9 months

First, it is doubtful that Melinda will be able to receive welfare if she moves out at age 16. If she can get money on her own, she and Holly may still have trouble renting an apartment.

Apartment owners often choose not to rent to young single mothers and their children, especially if they must rely on welfare for their income.

Second, Melinda doesn't appear to be planning realistically for her other expenses. She and Holly need to talk to other young families who live on their own. What do they actually spend for food? What about transportation? Clothing? Emergency expenses?

In some areas of the United States, apartments may rent for less than they do in California. However, in these areas AFDC payments are usually considerably lower.

*Parenting is expensive—and rewarding.*

The high cost of living independently may be unreal to you. Or that high cost may be the biggest reason you're still with your parents.

## Money Versus Happiness

Money doesn't buy happiness, but the lack of "enough" money can certainly cause a great deal of unhappiness. As you plan your future, it's important that you plan how you'll earn enough money to support your child.

Even if the two parents are together and both are working, they may have heavy financial problems:

*We had credit, and we got deeper and deeper in
debt. When we finally wrote it down in black and
white, we had $2600 debts each month, but we
brought in only $1900.*

*We wrote letters, trying to be rational. That didn't
help. They picked up all our furniture, and we filed
for bankruptcy a year ago.*

*It was hard on the kids when the furniture went.
We had no refrigerator. We slept on the floor on a
mattress and ate out of an icebox. How do you
explain that to kids?*

*After filing for bankruptcy, your credit is ruined for
seven to ten years. You have to get a co-signer or
have a lot of collateral in order to get credit.*

*We scrimp from week to week. We're just not
money managers at all. What we're trying now is for
Denver to hold the checkbook. He keeps it so I can't
write checks.*

*The worst thing you can do is to file for bank-
ruptcy. I would sell everything in my house before I'd
do that again.*

*I would go to a credit counselor, but Denver won't
go. He thinks we should be able to manage it
ourselves—but we're not.*

*It's just that hard. The important thing is to man-
age your money. I think we should be teaching money
management in the schools.*

Mitzi, 22 - Selene, 5; Vaughn, 2

Whatever your income, you might think about Mitzi's
last comment. Sometimes a class in money management
can help a person plan how best to budget her income.

If you think you're heading for financial trouble, get
help. Don't coast along until you have the big money
problems facing Mitzi, Denver, and their children.

You may be able to find a non-profit group offering credit counseling in your community. Be careful of credit counselors who charge big fees.

Look under "Debt Counseling" or a similar heading in your telephone directory. Try to find someone who, at little or no charge, will help you work out a plan to budget your income.

With some professional help, plus lots of effort on your part, you may be able to pull out of seemingly hopeless money problems.

## When You Have Other Problems

Of course not all problems come with dollar signs. Teen parents, like everyone else, have ups and downs in their lives.

You may already be in school or you may have a job. You may be making plans for your future and for your child's future. If, however, your life is not going the way you want it to go, have you considered getting extra help? You don't have to handle everything by yourself.

*It's hard being a single parent. We were living together for awhile, and I miss the emotional support.*
*When I get really uptight, I put Juanita in the crib and let her cry. There's nothing I can do unless I hold her all day, and then I'm more upset.*

Esperanza, 17 - Juanita, 12 months

If you're having more problems than you can handle by yourself, the first step is to accept the fact that you need help. Some people find it very hard to admit they aren't making it on their own.

You're probably already getting informal help. Families often are a good source of support. So are friends. In fact, other young parents can offer tremendous support simply because they're facing some of the same problems that are bothering you.

## Finding Community Resources

You may need help beyond what your family and friends can give. Perhaps they can suggest community resources for you to contact. Inquire about resources from other people with whom you interact—the director of a child-care center, your minister, doctor, or teacher.

Also check your telephone book. Your county or state Mental Health Association and Psychology Department at your local college may recommend counseling services.

If you're receiving AFDC (welfare), ask to see a social worker when you need special help. Social workers often have far too heavy case loads, but some are able to provide extra help to their clients.

If you have a local community center, the social worker there may be able to tell you where to go for help with your problems. Your hospital social service department may be a good resource.

More than 300 agencies in the United States are connected with the Family Service Association of America. These agencies offer individual and family counseling at low cost, as well as a variety of other family services.

For the agency in your area, check your telephone directory under the following listings: Family Service Association, Council for Community Services, County Department of Health, Counseling Clinic, Mental Health Clinic, or United Fund.

## Don't Give Up

Generally you can get a list of hot lines from your telephone operator. Dial "411," then say, "I have this type of problem. Can you help me?"

## *If a person answers your call but can't help, ask for referrals.*

You may find, as you call hot lines and other community services, that phone numbers you have been given are not helping you. Too often the number has been changed, your call is answered by a recording, or the person responding tells you that agency can't help you.

When this happens, don't give up. If a person answers your call but can't help, ask for referrals. Tell him/her you need help. You don't know where to call next. Explain how much you would appreciate any ideas s/he may give you.

## Pregnancy and Marital Counseling

If you're pregnant unexpectedly, your community probably has several agencies specifically organized to help you and others in your situation.

Call the Planned Parenthood Association, Florence Crittenton Services, Catholic Charities, or family or children's services. Or talk to your guidance counselor, your doctor, or your pastor.

If you are a single parent, find out if there is a support group for single parents in your community. Check with the above resources for information about such groups. In some areas, Children's Home Society sponsors single-parent support groups.

Marriage and family counselors are usually listed in the telephone yellow pages. Your community may have a cost-free counseling agency, or the cost may be based on your income. If you have very little income, you may not be charged a fee.

Independence and self-sufficiency are wonderful things—if they work. All of us need extra help at some time in our lives. If this is your time of special need, do whatever is necessary to get that help. Both you and your child will be glad you did.

## Writing Your Life Script

Some people feel that a young woman who has a child when she is 16 is doomed to a life of poverty and unhappiness. They point out that the young mother will probably drop out of school and won't be able to find a steady job, a job which pays enough to provide for herself and her child. She may feel she has to get married. Her life choices seem quite limited.

If a teenage parent can, however, continue her education, improve her vocational skills, find a job, and, when she is ready, marry someone she wants to marry, her life script can be quite different.

*You and your child
deserve the best there is.*

Most of the young women in this book are not settling for a life of hardship because of early childbearing. Instead, many are continuing their education and are acquiring job skills. They are *not* accepting a life script filled with poverty and unhappiness. They *are* finding that "writing" a successful life script is a difficult task.

Even a very young mother can be in charge of her life script . . . *if* she continues her education and acquires vocational skills. For most young mothers, this will be very difficult, but well worth the effort.

You and your child deserve the best there is. If you get your education and improve your vocational skills, *you* can be in charge of your life script.

*More power to you!*

# Appendix

# About The Author

Jeanne Warren Lindsay, M.A., C.H.E., developed and for sixteen years coordinated the Teen Mother Program, an alternative offered to pregnant and parenting students in the ABC Unified School District, Cerritos, California. This program is a choice offered to pregnant and parenting students who do not wish to attend the comprehensive high school throughout pregnancy. Ms. Lindsay has counseled hundreds of pregnant teenagers and teenage parents, and she continues as an active consultant in the program.

Ms. Lindsay has advanced degrees in home economics and anthropology. She edited the *NOAPP Network,* quarterly newsletter of the National Organization on Adolescent Pregnancy and Parenting, 1983-1990, and she currently edits *PPT Express,* a newsletter for teachers and others working with pregnant and parenting teens. She frequently gives presentations across the country on the culture of school-age parents, teaching parenting to teenage parents; educating pregnant and parenting teens, adoption, and other topics.

Ms. Lindsay is the author or co-author of thirteen other books on adolescent pregnancy and parenting, teenage marriage, and adoption from the birthfamily's perspective. Titles are listed on page 2.

Jeanne and Bob have been married for 40 years. They have five children and five gorgeous grandchildren.

# Bibliography

Dozens of books on parenting are published each year. Following are a few which may be of special interest to teenage parents. If you can't find a book you want in your bookstore, you usually can order it directly from the publisher. Enclose $2 for shipping in addition to price of the book.

Prices, when given, are from the 1990 edition of *Books in Print.*

Brazelton, T. Barry. *Toddlers and Parents.* 1989. 249 pp. Doubleday, 666 Fifth Avenue, NY, NY 10103.

> Brazelton's discussions of parenting are hard to beat. Beautiful photos.

Green, Martin I. *A Sigh of Relief: The First-Aid Handbook for Childhood Emergencies*. 1989. 264 pp. Bantam Books, 666 Fifth Avenue, New York, NY 10103.

> Lots of illustrations and information about all sorts of things. Easy to find suggestions for treating childhood emergencies.

Lansky, Vicki. *The Taming of the C.A.N.D.Y. Monster.* 1986. 121 pp. The Book Peddlers, 18326 Minnetonka Boulevard, Deephaven, MN 55391.

> An excellent cookbook for parents. Lots of recipes for healthful food for children. Tips for escaping the junk food trap.

Leach, Penelope. *Your Baby and Child from Birth to Age Five.* Revised, 1989. 554 pp. Alfred A. Knopf.

> An absolutely beautiful book packed with information, many color photos and lovely drawings. Comprehensive, authoritative, and outstandingly sensitive guide to child care and development.

Lindsay, Jeanne Warren. *Do I Have a Daddy? A Story About a Single-Parent Child.* 1991. 48 pp. Morning Glory Press.

> Picture story for child who doesn't know his/her father. Includes 16-page section with suggestions for single mothers. Beautifully illustrated by Cheryl Boeller.

_____. *Pregnant Too Soon: Adoption Is an Option.* 1988. 224 pp. Morning Glory Press.

> Personal stories of young birthmothers plus information on agency and independent adoption, fathers' rights, and other aspects of adoption.

_____. *School-Age Parents: The Challenge of Three-Generation Living.* 1990. 224 pp. Morning Glory Press.

> A much needed book for dealing with the frustrations, problems, and pleasures of three-generation living.

_____. *Teenage Marriage: Coping with Reality.* 1988. 208 pp. Morning Glory Press.

Marriage book written especially for teenagers. Based on in-depth interviews with married teens and on nationwide survey of more than 3000 teenagers' attitudes toward marriage.

_____. *Teens Parenting—Your Baby's First Year.* 1991. 192 pp. Morning Glory Press.

How-to-parent book especially for teenage parents of infants. It's the companion book to *Teens Parenting—The Challenge of Toddlers*. Lots more quotes from teenage parents who share their experiences with their children.

_____ and Jean Brunelli. *Teens Parenting—Your Pregnancy and Newborn Journey.* 1991. 192 pp. Morning Glory Press.

Prenatal health book for pregnant teenagers. Includes section on care of the newborn and a chapter for fathers.

_____ and Sally McCullough. *Teens Parenting—Discipline from Birth to Three.* 1991. 192 pp. Morning Glory Press.

Provides guidance for preventing and dealing with discipline problems with babies and toddlers. Lots of photos.

Maracek, Mary. *Say "No!" to Violence.* 1983. 48 pp. $6.00. Resolve, Inc. Available from Morning Glory Press.

Underlying message is that the reader does not deserve to be hit. Simply written. Can help a young woman escape an abusive relationship.

Peterson, Judy, Editor. *Inside-Outside.* Published quarterly. Inside-Outside, 4680 Lake Underhill, Orlando, FL 32807. 16 pp. per issue. Annual subscription, $15.00. 15-copy subscription, $35; 25-copy, $49.

Beautiful full-color quarterly magazine for teenage parents. Lots of photos.

***Parent Express Series.*** ANR Publications, University of
California, 6701 San Pablo Avenue, Oakland, CA
94608-1239. $3 per set payable to UC Regents.

> Wonderful series of newsletters for parents. The first set starts
> two months before delivery and continues through the first
> year of the child's life. Second set covers second and
> third years.

Segal, Marilyn, Ph.D., and Don Adcock, Ph.D. ***Your Child
at Play: One to Two Years.*** 1985. 224 pp. Paper,
$9.95. ***Your Child at Play: Two to Three Years.***
208 pp. 1985. Paper, $9.95.

> Provides a wonderful variety of activities for toddlers and their
> parents. Lots of photos.

Spock, Benjamin, M.D. ***Dr. Spock on Parenting.*** 1989.
224 pp. Paper, $4.95. Simon and Schuster, 1230
Avenue of the Americas, New York, NY 10020.

> Written in Dr. Spock's chatty way, it's a good book if you like
> to read and want a lot of information on all kinds of topics
> related to childrearing.

White, Burton L. ***The First Three Years of Life.*** 1990.
352 pp. Paper, $9.95. Prentice Hall.

> White stresses the importance of parenting during the first
> three years of a child's life.

# Index

## BOOKS FOR/ABOUT PREGNANT/PARENTING TEENS

*TEENS PARENTING—Your Pregnancy and Newborn Journey*
How to take care of yourself and your newborn. For pregnant teens.

*TEENS PARENTING—Your Baby's First Year*
*TEENS PARENTING—The Challenge of Toddlers*
Two how-to-parent books especially for teenage parents.

*TEENS PARENTING—Discipline from Birth to Three*
How to prevent and deal with discipline problems with babies/toddlers.

*SCHOOL-AGE PARENTS: Challenge of Three-Generation Living*
Written to families whose teen brings her (or his) baby home to live.
Excellent guidance for those struggling with three-generation living.

*SURVIVING TEEN PREGNANCY: Choices, Dreams, and Decisions*
For all pregnant teens—help with decisions, moving on toward goals.

*PREGNANT TOO SOON: Adoption Is an Option*
Advocates choice. Young birthmothers tell their stories.

*TEENAGE MARRIAGE: Coping with Reality*
Gives teenagers a picture of the realities of marriage.

*TEENS LOOK AT MARRIAGE: Rainbows, Roles and Reality*
Describes the research behind *Teenage Marriage.*

*ADOPTION AWARENESS: A Guide for Teachers, Nurses,*
*Counselors and Caring Others*
Guide for supporting adoption alternative in crisis pregnancy.

*PARENTS, PREGNANT TEENS AND THE ADOPTION OPTION*
For all parents who feel alone as their daughter faces too-early
pregnancy and the difficult adoption/keeping decision.

*DO I HAVE A DADDY? A Story About a Single-Parent Child*
Picture/story book especially for children with only one parent.
Includes special sixteen-page section for single parent.

*OPEN ADOPTION: A Caring Option*
A fascinating and sensitive account of the new world of adoption.

*TEEN PREGNANCY CHALLENGE, Book One: Strategies for*
*Change; Book Two: Programs for Kids*
Book One provides practical guidelines for developing adolescent
pregnancy prevention and care programs. Book Two focuses on
programs all along the adolescent pregnancy prevention continuum.

**Please see ordering information on back of page.**

# MORNING GLORY PRESS

6595 San Haroldo Way, Buena Park, CA 90620
714/828-1998 — FAX 714/828-2049

Please send me the following:

| Quantity | Price | Total |
|---|---|---|
| *Surviving Teen Pregnancy* | | |
| Paper, ISBN 0-930934-47-4 | $9.95 | |
| Cloth, ISBN 0-930934-46-6 | 15.95 | |
| *School-Age Parents: Coping with Three-Generation Living* | | |
| ____Paper, ISBN 0-930934-36-9 | 10.95 | |
| ____Cloth, ISBN 0-930934-37-7 | 17.95 | |
| *Teens Parenting—Your Pregnancy and Newborn Journey* | | |
| ____Paper, ISBN 0-930934-50-4 | 9.95 | |
| ____Cloth, ISBN 0-930934-51-2 | 15.95 | |
| *Teens Parenting—Your Baby's First Year* | | |
| ____Paper, ISBN 0-930934-52-0 | 9.95 | |
| ____Cloth, ISBN 0-930934-53-9 | 15.95 | |
| *Teens Parenting—Challenge of Toddlers* | | |
| ____Paper, ISBN 0-930934-58-x | 9.95 | |
| ____Cloth, ISBN 0-930934-59-8 | 15.95 | |
| *Teens Parenting—Discipline from Birth to Three* | | |
| ____Paper, ISBN 0-930934-54-7 | 9.95 | |
| ____Cloth, ISBN 0-930934-55-5 | 15.95 | |
| *Teen Pregnancy Challenge, Book 1: Strategies for Change* | | |
| ____Paper, ISBN 0-930934-34-2 | 14.95 | |
| ____Cloth, ISBN 0-930934-35-0 | 19.95 | |
| *Teen Pregnancy Challenge, Book 2: Programs for Kids* | | |
| ____Paper, ISBN 0-930934-38-5 | 14.95 | |
| ____Cloth, ISBN 0-930934-39-3 | 19.95 | |
| ____*Pregnant Too Soon: Adoption Is an Option* | 9.95 | |
| ____*Open Adoption: A Caring Option* | 9.95 | |
| ____*Adoption Awareness: A Guide for Teachers, Counselors, Nurses, and Caring Others* | 12.95 | |
| ____*Parents, Pregnant Teens and the Adoption Option* | 8.95 | |
| ____*Teenage Marriage: Coping with Reality* | 9.95 | |
| ____*Teens Look at Marriage* | 9.95 | |
| ____*Do I Have a Daddy?* | 5.95 | |
| **TOTAL** | | |

**Please add postage: 1-3 bks., $2.50; 4+, 75¢/book**
**California residents add 7.75% sales tax**

**TOTAL**

Ask about quantity discounts, Teacher, Student Guides.
Prepayment requested. School/library purchase orders accepted.
If not satisfied, return in 15 days for refund.

NAME _____

ADDRESS _____